EATING IN WITH
JAMES MARTIN

Dedication

I would like to dedicate this book to my family for all their support, both loving and financial, over the last 25 years; my agents Linda and Fiona for keeping me so busy over the past year and for helping me to afford a decent car; to Ken Allanson, my old course tutor from Scarborough College; and Anthony Worrall Thompson for being there as a friend and teaching me the real art of good food.

First published in Great Britain in 1998 by
Mitchell Beazley, an imprint of Octopus
Publishing Group Ltd

Reprinted 2001, 2002, 2003, 2004

This edition published in 2007 by Bounty Books,
a division of Octopus Publishing Group Ltd
2–4 Heron Quays, London E14 4JP

An Hachette Livre UK Company

ISBN: 978-0-753715-80-2

A CIP catalogue record for this book is available from the British Library

The author and publishers will be grateful for any information which will assist them in keeping future editions up to date. Although all reasonable care has been taken in the preparation of this book, neither the publishers nor the author can accept any liability for any consequences arising from the use thereof, or the information contained herein

Written in association with Susan Fleming
Commissioning Editor: Margaret Little
Executive Art Editor: Fiona Knowles
Editor: Margot Richardson
Photography: Jeremy Hopley, assisted by Catherine Rowlands
Stylist: Wei Tang
Food Prop Buyer: Meg Janz
Production: Rachel Lynch
Clothing supplied by Cadogans of Winchester. Furniture supplied by Coexistance, London

Printed and bound in China

EATING IN WITH
JAMES MARTIN

Bounty
Books

contents

finger food

light meals

foreword

One of the most rewarding aspects of being a chef is seeing a young chef who you 'spotted' develop into serious talent. That chef for me is James Martin. I first saw James when I, and other chefs including Brian Turner, were judging students at Scarborough College. From the moment I saw his cooking skills I knew that this guy had star qualities. I had no hesitation in offering him a job when he finished his cookery course, and he accepted a *commis* chef's position at 190 Queen's Gate.

James Martin's decision to brave the crazy world of London restaurants couldn't have been easy, but, along with most of what he has done since, he took it in his stride. For weeks I don't think he knew what had hit him. It wasn't long after he joined us that due to the usual staffing problems, he found himself running the restaurant's pastry section. It was a busy restaurant and this enforced maturity could have broken many a young chef. But not James – he went from strength to strength.

The sad day arrived when James wanted to move on, a necessity for any young chef who naturally wants to develop all his talents. I didn't stand in his way and wished him well, knowing full well that I would encounter him again later in life. James followed an excellent training route. The success of the Hotel and Bistro du Vin's restaurant, with a waiting list of many weeks, must surely be down to his brilliance in the kitchen.

It wasn't long before his other talents, combined with his cooking, were spotted by the television companies. His good looks and charm made him a natural for television.

It gave me a great feeling of satisfaction when he succeeded in becoming a *Ready Steady Cook* chef. His first challenge on the programme was against me. Yes, you guessed it, he won. No hard feelings. James was on his way, and it couldn't happen to a nicer guy.

Eating in with James Martin encompasses all that is good in modern cookbooks. He has grasped the need for simplicity, realizing that not many of us have time for marathon sessions in the kitchen. You will find his recipes quick and simple with fabulous results. The food we eat today shouldn't stand on ceremony. It needs to be simple to prepare and the recipes need to be easy to understand.

Gone are the days of competing with the Joneses, sending out private invitations, getting out the best china, polishing the silver and going O.T.T. This is 'mates' food, a little snack here, a cocktail there, dinner for two, family fodder, exciting explosions of taste.

James Martin has analyzed how he likes to eat and created a recipe book he knows you'll enjoy. Too many chefs give you recipes for food that they think you *should* eat rather than food that you actually *want* to eat. James Martin doesn't make that mistake. He offers you tips, little cheats and a wealth of information that will make your life in the kitchen that little bit easier. He has removed wordly boundaries, encompassing food that he has enjoyed from his travels, but always remembering to adapt the recipes to suit what you might buy in your weekly shopping list.

Get stuck in. After reading this book, you'll feel it's safe to go back into the kitchen.

introduction

This book is about the pleasures of eating at home. It contains over a
hundred of my favourite recipes for those who, like me, enjoy cooking
and eating, but don't have much time to spare. Home cooking shouldn't
be hard work, involving twenty ingredients, ten pans and a sink full of
washing up, but should follow my four main culinary rules: to be relaxed,
quick, simple and different. However, flavour is a prime consideration as
well – so much so that it has become a separate 'rule' all on its own.

To be relaxed about cooking is vital, and I've borne this in mind in
all the recipes, which are for good honest food, but with an innovative
touch. I've taken both traditional and new ideas and combined them in a
way that appeals first to the taste-buds, then to the eye – and all without
too much hard graft. Some dishes can be created in seconds, some in a
few minutes, and most take less than an hour to prepare and cook. You
should never have to spend hours in the kitchen when cooking for friends
or family at home.

Food should be kept simple as well, but at the same time I try
to introduce new tastes and create exciting and different flavour
combinations. There are quite a few dishes here that are *almost*
traditional, but which have a little twist of imagination that transforms
them into something new and fresh.

Often it is the ingredients themselves that are different. I always start with good-quality ingredients – the best meat, fish, vegetables and oils – because they are the basis of good cooking and eating. But I have also used a number of ready-prepared supermarket foods which, when incorporated into a dish, can be as good as if not better than fresh ingredients. I'm talking here about things such as tins of tomatoes or pulses, bought pastry and baked goods, and frozen peas or beans. Their contribution to flavour is important, but the fact that they also save time is central to my culinary philosophy.

'Why home cooking?' you might ask. Well, I'm a trained chef, but home is where I first encountered and started to appreciate the joys of food. I grew up on a farm in Yorkshire. Helping my mother prepare Sunday lunch from about the age of eight – standing on a stool to stir the gravy – is a strong early memory. My grandparents, too, let me in on a few old home-cooking secrets, not least what to do with left-overs. As my father was in charge of the catering at Castle Howard, the most beautiful stately home in Yorkshire, I suppose you could say that an interest in food was inevitable. As a result, quite a number of the recipes included here are old family favourites.

Despite failing my GCSE in cookery – yes, it's true! – I went on to train at Scarborough Technical College where I learned the basics of my chosen profession from Ken Allanson, a superb teacher. It was there too that I was 'discovered' by Antony Worrall Thompson, who has since been the greatest influence in my life. I worked with him in London for a while, then he advised me to go to the Continent to learn what I could from other cuisines. Although I worked in a few restaurants in France, I spent most time in the kitchens of some of the great Bordeaux châteaux. This was traditional cookery at its best, on a fairly large scale, and I learned an enormous amount.

Back home, I worked as pastry chef at Chewton Glen, in my view the best hotel in Europe, then moved to be head chef at the Hotel du Vin in Winchester – and I was still only twenty-one! Once more I cooked good honest bistro-type food, more homely in style than the culinary heights I had just experienced but with a twist of originality. Television lured me away from there after three happy years – *Ready Steady Cook* must be the best training ground for producing good food quickly!

I've come a long way in a very short time, and I've cooked at the very highest levels, but at heart I'm still most enthusiastic about good food that you can cook at home. Armed with some of the short cuts, corner-cutting hints and chefs' secrets outlined in the following chapters, I hope you too will be able to cook great food that's relaxed, quick, simple and different.

Whether you're cooking up a storm for a party, planning a romantic dinner or simply getting some friends together for an impromptu lunch or supper, have a great time!

James

finger food

Finger food is something that people usually eat at the same time as having a drink. This could vary from a bowl of nachos and a beer when staying in with friends, to a few slightly more elaborate offerings for a full-fledged party.

We all know we should eat something while we drink alcohol. Many a hangover has been worse because nothing was eaten the night before. However, don't mistake the motivation of pubs and bars in offering bowls of salted nuts or salty crisps: they're not being kind, they're trying to get you to drink more!

The sort of food I like to eat with my fingers is not the fiddly canapés you get at posh drinks parties. They take hours to prepare and are not very satisfying when you eat them. I like to *really* eat something at a party – whether it's for four or forty – and appreciate chunks of proper food. A piece of garlic bread or wedge of pizza, or some crudités or breadsticks to plunge into a bowl of tasty dip is much more my style.

That's the sort of thing you'll find in this first chapter. The recipes are quick to prepare and serve: none will take you longer than ten minutes to make, from start to finish. All the ingredients are easy to find, and some basic components can be bought ready-prepared in jars or tins at a supermarket. What could be simpler and quicker than blitzing a couple of tins of chickpeas and a tin of roasted red peppers together with a few other flavours? The Roasted Red Pepper Hummus on page 15 is stunning to look at and delicious to eat.

The recipes here could also be described as on-the-move food. Take a number of them on a picnic or as a packed lunch. A couple of the recipes could even work as a starter for a meal.

Whatever your taste, these dishes are all to do with saving both time and effort, serving things simply in bowls and not spending hours on presentation and making them look pretty.

Camembert and Garlic Bread

1 large oven-ready garlic baguette or 4 thick slices fresh sourdough bread

2 garlic cloves, peeled and finely chopped

115 g (4 oz) butter, softened

175 g (6 oz) Camembert cheese, sliced

Some people say garlic is the root of all evil. But for me, garlic is heaven. This bread can be made in the 'proper' chef's way using a good-quality bread plus butter and garlic; or the cheat's way with ready-made garlic bread. To be honest, though, there isn't much difference in the time taken: 'cheating' just involves less work.

Sourdough is the best bread for this recipe, a bread eaten in the eastern parts of Europe, in Russia and in America. It is raised by a leaven of flour and water that is left to ferment, utilizing natural yeasts in the flour to create gases which raise the dough and give it a unique sour flavour. If you can't find any good sourdough, use *pain de campagne*, a French country bread available from most supermarkets.

Cheat's method *Take the oven-ready garlic bread and bake in the oven following the instructions on the packet (normally for about 10 minutes, at about 180°C/350°F/gas mark 4). Remove from the oven, cover with slices of the cheese, and place under a pre-heated grill until the cheese just melts. Don't worry if the edges burn: they are the best bits.*

Sourdough method *Mix the garlic with the butter. Toast the sourdough bread, then spread the garlic butter on it. Cover with cheese as above, and grill until the cheese has just melted.*

Mozzarella and Parmesan Pizza

1 x 35 cm (14 in) medium
thickness ready-made
pizza base

100 g (3½ oz) Parmesan,
freshly grated

200 g (7 oz) buffalo
Mozzarella cheese

Olive oil

Rock salt and freshly
ground black pepper

A very simple pizza, which is good eaten with a tomato
and basil salad, or cut into wedges as finger food.

It is important to use Mozzarella made from buffalo
milk that comes in whey in a plastic bag. It is creamier
and richer than the cow's milk versions which are
rubbery and bland, and it has a far superior flavour.

1 Pre-heat the oven to 220°C/425°F/gas mark 7. Using a
sharp knife, carefully cut the pizza base in half horizontally
to make two thin, round pizza bases.

2 Sprinkle the grated Parmesan evenly over the two bases.
Cut the Mozzarella into thin slices and arrange on the top.
Drizzle with olive oil, season well with salt and pepper, and
bake for about 5–10 minutes until golden brown.

Roasted Red Pepper Hummus

2 x 400 g (14 oz) tins
chickpeas

1 x 400 g (14 oz) tin or jar
roasted red peppers

3 garlic cloves,
peeled and chopped

1 x 15 g (½ oz) packet
fresh mint

4–5 tablespoons sesame oil

Salt and freshly ground
black pepper

Hummus is a traditional Middle Eastern dip made from
chickpeas and sesame *tahina*, but my variation contains
roasted red peppers to give it a different and more
interesting flavour. I love red peppers, and don't really
use any of the other colours as they never seem to taste
of anything when puréed.

This hummus is very simple to make, and is best
served with hot miniature pitta breads, breadsticks or
crudités of carrot, celery and red pepper.

1 Drain the chickpeas and peppers in a sieve.
2 Put the chickpeas, peppers, garlic and mint into a food
processor and blend until smooth.
3 Stir in the sesame oil and season to taste with salt and
pepper. Spoon into a bowl.

James's tip
*Using tinned chickpeas saves time, and once they're
puréed they taste no different from dried, cooked ones.
Tinned roasted peppers are fairly new in supermarkets,
but are also available in good delicatessens.*

Deep-fried Parsnip Chips

2 large firm parsnips,
trimmed and scrubbed

Oil for deep-frying

Salt

This snack, ideal with a drink, is served in some of London's trendy bars. It is very simple to make. You can use other vegetables instead of or as well as the parsnips, such as carrots, beetroots, courgettes and, of course, potatoes. A mixture of different vegetables in a bowl would look and taste great.

The chips can also be used to garnish main course dishes, as can deep-fried herbs which are also tasty as a finger food, especially when sprinkled with salt and toasted sesame seeds.

1 Put the oil in a deep pan, and heat until very hot. If possible, use a metal basket as it makes it easier to move the chips around and lift them out of the oil.
2 Using a potato peeler, peel long strips of parsnip, skin and all, down the length of the vegetable.
3 Carefully place a handful of the parsnip strips in the oil and keep moving the basket to stop them sticking. When the parsnips are a light golden colour, not brown, remove and drain on some kitchen paper.
4 Season with a little salt, and keep warm while you deep-fry the remaining parsnip chips.

finger food

17

Mango, Mint and Red Chilli Salsa

1 large ripe mango

¼ small red onion,
peeled and finely diced

½ fresh red chilli,
de-seeded and finely diced
(see page 137)

**1 x 15 g (½ oz) packet fresh
mint,** chopped

2 tablespoons olive oil

**Salt and freshly ground
black pepper**

Mangos are one of the most versatile of fruits and can be served both as a dessert and with meat and chicken dishes. (Try them just plain with some fresh lime juice and chopped mint – great for breakfast.)

When I worked as the sauce chef at 190 Queen's Gate, the superb London restaurant run by Antony Worrall Thompson, this dish was one of the most popular on the menu. It was served with roast duck, but it can be eaten as a salsa or on a crostini: a slice of Italian bread, usually *ciabatta*, which has been briefly roasted or toasted. It is also fabulous with cold cooked chicken or salmon.

1 Remove the skin from the mango carefully, making sure not to take too much of the flesh away in the process. Cut all the flesh away from the large stone, then cut it into 1 cm (½ in) cubes.

2 Put the mango pieces in a bowl. Add the onion, chilli, chopped mint and olive oil. Season with salt and pepper and mix well.

James's tip

If a mango (or avocado) is unripe when you buy it, wrap it in newspaper and leave somewhere warm for a day or so. It will ripen up well.

Red Onion and Crème Fraîche Tart

1 x 375 g (13 oz) packet
ready-made puff pastry,
cut in half

1 tablespoon olive oil

6 red onions,
peeled and thinly sliced

1 sprig fresh thyme

Salt and freshly ground
black pepper

200 ml (7 fl oz) crème
fraîche

This is an unusual tart, in which the ingredients are prepared separately, and then brought together at the last minute. Cut into squares to offer as finger food.

I use ready-made puff pastry. Most chefs, if they are honest, use this as it saves so much messing around (and a nagging pastry chef in the kitchen).

This pastry and filo pastry are great convenience foods. Puff is normally available frozen, but can sometimes be bought fresh, which tastes much better but has a shorter shelf life.

1   Pre-heat the oven to 200°C/400°F/gas mark 6. Roll out the two pastry pieces until they are about 5mm (¼ in) thick and about 30 cm (12 in) in diameter, and place on greased oven trays. Prick very well all over with a fork and place in the oven for 10–15 minutes until coloured and cooked through.

2   Put the oil in a pan and heat. Add the onion, thyme leaves and a little salt and pepper. Cook until soft: about 20 minutes.

3   Spread the crème fraîche thinly on to the puff pastry bases, and cover with the onions. Serve hot or cold.

James's tip

Pricking the pastry prevents it from rising which may seem like a waste of puff pastry, but the texture is more solid, making it useful as a base, and the taste is divine. You could also put another baking tray on top of the pastry to make sure it doesn't rise.

finger food

19

Green-pea Guacamole with Nachos

450 g (1 lb) frozen peas

½ small red onion,
peeled and finely chopped

1 garlic clove,
peeled and finely chopped

10 mint leaves

115 g (4 oz) plain yoghurt

½ fresh red chilli,
de-seeded and finely
chopped (see page 137)

1 teaspoon ground cumin

Salt and freshly ground
black pepper

Olive oil

To serve

I large bag nachos

Frozen peas have a superb flavour and require very little cooking. Here, they are not cooked at all, just defrosted to make a quick dip or spread.

This recipe can also serve as a salsa, and is particularly good with grilled or barbecued *merguez*, the hot, spicy, thin sausages from Algeria. Found in delicatessens, good butchers and some supermarkets, be careful when cooking them as they smoke a lot due to the amount of fat they contain.

If you don't like dips that are too spicy, leave out the chilli, but do keep the cumin – using a little more perhaps – as this complements the flavour of the peas.

1   Defrost the peas, and thoroughly drain off any water.
2   Place the peas in a food processor together with the onion, garlic and mint, and purée slightly. Add the yoghurt, and purée again.
3   Remove from the mixer and stir in the chilli and ground cumin. Add salt and pepper to taste.
4   Place in a bowl, drizzle some olive oil on the top, and dig in with the nachos.

James's tip

If you do not have a food processor at home, use a hand-operated vegetable mill, or a mortar and pestle. Alternatively, you can crush the peas with a potato masher before mixing with everything else; this makes for a much coarser texture.

'These dishes are all to do with saving both time and effort, a cause very close to my culinary heart...'

Red Pepper Fritters
with Garlic Mayonnaise

2 red peppers

Oil for deep-frying

Salt and freshly ground
black pepper

Batter

150 g (5½ oz) self-raising
flour

250 ml (9 fl oz) good bitter
or ale

1 x 15 g (½ oz) packet fresh
coriander leaves, chopped

Garlic mayonnaise

200 ml (7 fl oz) mayonnaise

1 tablespoon garlic purée

This is a dish I made for *Ready Steady Cook* on television, and which is a great hit as a drinks snack in restaurants where I have worked.

A batter for deep-frying can be made in a number of ways – plain, with yeast or with baking powder – but using beer gives good flavour and makes the batter crisp up very well. This batter can also be used to deep-fry fish, fruit, or other vegetables such as carrot, courgette and aubergine. You could even combine a selection of vegetable fritters to serve with this or any other relevant dip. Try other mayonnaise flavours as well, such as rocket and lemon.

1 Cut the peppers in half, remove the seeds and stalks, and slice them into 2 cm (¾ in) strips.
2 Heat the oil in a deep-fryer or deep pan to a high heat.
3 To make the batter, place the flour in a bowl, season well and slowly add the beer, mixing well with a whisk. Add the chopped coriander. The batter should be thick and glutinous.
4 Dip the pepper strips in the batter, let any excess drip away, and deep-fry in batches until golden brown. Remove and place on some kitchen paper to drain, then season with a little salt.
5 Mix the mayonnaise with the garlic purée and place in a bowl on a platter. Arrange the fritters around the bowl. Eat them just warm, dipped in the mayonnaise.

Jumbo Prawns with Rocket Mayonnaise

10 large cooked prawns

1 x 15 g (½ oz) packet fresh
basil

85 g (3 oz) rocket leaves

Juice of 1 lime

200 ml (7 fl oz) mayonnaise

Salt and freshly ground
black pepper

A quick, no-frills snack or starter. Buy large prawns, usually available from supermarket fish counters. They are expensive, but are normally fresh rather than frozen. Due to their size they are easier to pick up and dip into the mayonnaise.

Rocket has become very popular, as it should, because it tastes great. Try to buy it in bunches from a greengrocer as it's much cheaper than buying it as a herb in packets at a supermarket.

1 Prepare the prawns by peeling them from the tail up to the head. Try to keep the head attached as they look better when kept whole.
2 In a food processor, purée half the basil and all the rocket together until smooth. Add the lime juice and mix into the mayonnaise. Season well with salt and pepper and place into a bowl on a serving dish.
3 Place the prawns around the bowl, and garnish with the rest of the fresh basil in sprigs.

Devils on Horseback

6 chicken livers

55 g (2 oz) butter

Salt and freshly ground
black pepper

Cayenne pepper

12 stoned ready-to-eat
prunes

6 rashers good smoked
streaky bacon, cut in half

I love to take traditional recipes and give them a twist. Here I've put chicken livers inside prunes, instead of the usual stuffing of almonds. Chicken livers are cheap, very tasty, and easy to cook in dishes such as this, or in pâtés or stuffings. They are also great in stews and casseroles for added flavour. Cook them to pink only, as overcooked liver is as tough as old boots.

1 To prepare the livers, trim away any excess stringy sinew, and any yellow-coloured parts. Cut the livers in half. Wash and pat dry.

2 In a hot pan, sauté the livers quickly in the butter for about 1 minute until just sealed, seasoning them with salt and pepper. Remove from the pan and dust with cayenne pepper; as much or as little as you like.

3 Stuff each prune with a half liver, then wrap up in the bacon strips and secure with wooden cocktail sticks.

4 Place under a pre-heated grill until the bacon is crisp, about 1–2 minutes on each side. If you allow the 'devils' to cool slightly, you can remove the cocktail sticks without them falling apart.

'I love British food,
    but in my travels I've encountered
many new ideas and ingredients
            which have since
    become part of my repertoire'

Baba Ganoush

2 large aubergines

Olive oil

2 tablespoons light *tahina*

3 garlic cloves,
peeled and chopped

10 walnut halves

Juice and zest of 1 lemon

1 x 15 g (½ oz) packet fresh
mint

Salt and freshly ground
black pepper

This aubergine purée, made with *tahina*, a sesame seed paste, is ideal cold as a dip, or served hot as a garnish for lamb. Chefs who go in for fancy recipe titles call this 'aubergine caviar'. I much prefer its original Arabic name, which apparently means 'spoilt old man'. Mint and lemon are the predominant flavours here, but coriander and lime could be used for a change.

1 Cut the aubergines in half lengthways. Cut slits into the flesh in a zig-zag fashion, but do not pierce the skin.

2 In a hot pan, cook the aubergines in 1 cm (½ in) olive oil, flesh side down first for about 2 minutes. Then turn over and cook on the other side until soft and tender.

3 Place the aubergine flesh and skin, plus the *tahina*, garlic, walnuts, lemon and mint, into a food processor or blender. Purée until smooth.

4 Season well, and serve with a salad or with breadsticks.

James's tip

Lightly warmed through, the Baba Ganoush is wonderful served with charred or seared salmon. It's also good served cold with some cold cooked salmon.

Roasted Peppers Marinated in Balsamic Vinegar and Herbs

1 red pepper

1 green pepper

1 yellow pepper

Olive oil

¼ red onion, peeled and finely diced

2 garlic cloves, peeled and finely diced

75 ml (2½ fl oz) balsamic vinegar

1–2 x 15 g (½ oz) packets Italian herbs, chopped

Salt and freshly ground black pepper

Try this piled on to some charred bread, or just eaten on its own with a fork as part of an *antipasto*. If cut into chunks instead of strips, the peppers make a good garnish for hot cooked salmon, charred smoked salmon or cold chicken. If you decant the peppers into jam jars, they make a great present.

Packets of Italian herbs usually contain the soft herbs oregano, basil, tarragon and flat-leaf parsley.

1 Pre-heat the oven to 220°C/425°F/gas mark 7. Halve the peppers, remove the seeds and stalks, and place the halves on an ovenproof tray. Drizzle with olive oil and place in the oven until the skin is well coloured: about 15–20 minutes. Remove from the oven, and while the peppers are still hot, put them in a bowl and cover with clingfilm.

2 Mix the onion and garlic with 50 ml (2 fl oz) olive oil, the vinegar and chopped mixed herbs. Season with salt and pepper and leave to one side.

3 When the peppers are cool, peel off the skins and cut the flesh into 2 cm (¾ in) strips. Place in the marinade and season well. Eat straightaway or keep in the fridge for up to 24 hours.

James's tip

Using clingfilm to cover the bowl of peppers traps any steam which encourages the skin to rise up off the flesh. This is much quicker and less messy than burning the skins off over a naked flame. If you don't have enough time to roast them yourself, buy two 400 g (14 oz) tins or jars of roasted red peppers.

Hot Croissants with Sun-dried Tomatoes and Melted Cheese

4 croissants

¼ red onion, peeled and chopped

1 garlic clove, peeled and chopped

2 field mushrooms, wiped and sliced

25 g (1 oz) butter

8 sun-dried tomatoes in oil, drained

2 tablespoons chopped fresh parsley

Salt and freshly ground black pepper

225 g (8 oz) cheese, sliced (see above)

This is a good cheap dish, especially when made with slightly stale croissants, sometimes available on the discount shelves of supermarkets. For finger food for a party, cut the filled croissants carefully in half or into chunks or wedges.

You can use any cheese that goes runny when cooked. Camembert or Taleggio would be suitable. Camembert is widely available, but you might have to look a little harder for the latter – an Italian soft cow's milk cheese. It has a pinky-orange rind, is a little like Brie in texture and is well worth searching for.

Serve the croissants on their own or, if you're feeling hungry, with some grilled streaky bacon. Then lock the door and eat all four croissants. I do!

1 Pre-heat the oven to 180°C/350°F/gas mark 4. Cut the croissants in half horizontally and place the bottoms on an ovenproof tray, leaving the tops to one side.

2 Sauté the onion, garlic and mushrooms in the butter for about 1 minute, then add the tomatoes and the parsley. Season well.

3 Spread the onion mix on the four croissant bottoms on the tray, top with the cheese and put the four croissant lids on top. Place in the oven for 3–4 minutes just to lightly warm through and melt the cheese.

Antipasto of
Plum and Sun-dried Tomatoes

1 x 200 g (7 oz) jar
sun-dried tomatoes in oil

4 fresh plum tomatoes,
quartered

½ red onion,
peeled and thinly sliced

2 garlic cloves,
peeled and thinly sliced

1 tablespoon pesto sauce

1 x 15 g (½ oz) packet fresh
basil

Salt and freshly ground
black pepper

A great speedy topping for toast that can double up as a starter or as a garnish for a simple piece of roast cod. Puréed, it's also good as a dip, or stirred into some hot cooked pasta.

With so many varieties of tomato around these days, it's difficult to know what to choose. A real tomato rule of thumb is that fruit grown in hot countries, particularly those grown outside, will have much more flavour. Tomatoes sold or ripened on the vine may be more expensive, but they too will taste better because they have not been artificially ripened after picking.

1   Tip the sun-dried tomatoes into a pan. Add the fresh tomato quarters, onion, garlic and pesto.
2   Place on the heat to warm gently for 1 minute only. If you cook it for too long it will turn into a mush.
3   Remove from the heat. Tear the basil into pieces and add to the tomatoes. Season and serve. What could possibly be quicker?

Sun-dried Tomato Tapenade
with Breadsticks

1 x 400 g (14 oz) jar
sun-dried tomatoes in oil

1 tablespoon capers

2 tinned anchovy fillets

1 tablespoon pesto sauce

1 tablespoon pine kernels

Salt and freshly ground
black pepper

Olive oil (If necessary)

To serve

1 packet thin breadsticks

This is very easy to make and is a good dip for a drinks party. It uses sun-dried tomatoes instead of olives which is ideal for those who, like me, don't like olives. But it can be used in the same way as a traditional *tapenade*: as a spread, a stuffing, or an addition to sauces. It's good with lamb, chicken and fish.

1   Place all the ingredients into a food processor, except for the olive oil (but including the oil from the tomatoes). Blend until smooth. If there is enough oil in the tomatoes you shouldn't need any extra, but add a little more olive oil if the mixture seems too dry.
2   Turn into a bowl and serve on a dish surrounded by breadsticks.

Tartlets of Salmon Rillettes with Coriander

140 g (5 oz) cooked salmon
without skin and bone

55 g (2 oz) butter,
softened

¼ red onion,
peeled and finely diced

½ red pepper,
de-seeded and finely diced

1 garlic clove,
peeled and finely diced

Salt and freshly ground
black pepper

1 x 15 g (½ oz) packet fresh
coriander, chopped

1 packet (usually 24) small
savoury tartlet cases

No-one likes waste, and I love inventing recipes at home which use up leftover pieces of meat or fish. This is an ideal way of using up salmon (or you can buy cooked salmon fillets in most supermarkets). Tartlet cases are not essential; you could just spread the rillettes on some hot toast for a great finger-food snack.

1 Flake the salmon flesh in a bowl. Mix it with the softened butter, onion, pepper and garlic. Season well with salt and pepper. Add the chopped coriander.
2 Mix well and spoon into the tartlets. Serve fairly quickly as the tartlet cases will soften.

James's tip

The salmon mixture can be made the day before and stored in the fridge. Remove well before serving to allow it to soften slightly before spooning into the tartlet cases.

Smoked Mackerel Pâté with Char-grilled Courgettes

2 courgettes

Olive oil

Salt and freshly ground
black pepper

2 tablespoons pesto sauce

1 tablespoon pine kernels,
toasted

Juice and zest of 1 lemon

1 x 250 g (9 oz) tub
smoked mackerel pâté

Few sprigs fresh basil

This is a no-fuss dish using bought pâté with the simple flavour of grilled courgettes. The courgettes must be grilled on a griddle pan (see page 140) – not under a grill – as this gives them essential colour, texture and flavour.

1 Pre-heat a griddle pan to a high temperature.
2 Cut the courgettes in half lengthways, drizzle with olive oil and season with salt and pepper. Griddle the courgettes on both sides and leave to cool. Cut into bite-sized chunks.
3 Mix the pesto, pine kernels, lemon juice and zest and about a tablespoon of olive oil together, then season with salt and pepper. Leave to one side.
4 Place the chunks of courgette on a plate, and put a spoonful of pâté on top. Just before serving, add a spoonful of the pesto dressing. Garnish with sprigs of fresh basil around the edge.

Garlic Mushrooms and Taleggio Cheese on Toast

2 garlic cloves, peeled and crushed

55 g (2 oz) butter

1 x 15 g (½ oz) packet Italian herbs, chopped

4 large field mushrooms, sliced

Salt and freshly ground black pepper

Juice and zest of 1 lemon

2 slices white bloomer bread, toasted

55 g (2 oz) Taleggio cheese

Fresh thyme, chopped (optional)

As my mother would say, this is just poncey cheese on toast. However, to make a more sophisticated snack you could cut the mushrooms into smaller pieces, cook them as below, spoon into bought savoury tartlet cases, top with the Taleggio cheese and warm through in the oven.

1 Mix the garlic, butter and herbs together, and place in a hot pan with the sliced mushrooms. Season well. Cook quickly as the mushrooms tend to leak a lot of water otherwise. Add the lemon juice and zest.

2 Spread on the toasted bread. Top with the cheese and grill to just melt the cheese. Serve hot with some chopped fresh thyme if you have any. Cut into quarters to serve as chunky canapés.

James's tip

The pan must be really hot when cooking the mushrooms, otherwise the water in the mushrooms will leak out, diluting the flavours and making the bread soggy. If it does get a bit wet, 2 tablespoons of fresh breadcrumbs will soak it all up.

finger food

Hot Stilton Rarebit

25 g (1 oz) butter

3 egg yolks

1 teaspoon English mustard

90 ml (3 fl oz) ale or lager

Tabasco sauce

Worcestershire sauce

Salt and freshly ground
black pepper

225 g (8 oz) Stilton cheese,
grated

4 slices toast

Tomatoes, sliced (optional)

Rarebits or rabbits are centuries old, and were traditionally served as a savoury before or instead of a sweet. They are usually made with Cheddar or Caerphilly cheese, but Stilton gives a much stronger flavour. You can use the leftovers from cans of beer, but don't replace the beer with milk as some recipes suggest, as this ruins the taste.

1 Pre-heat the grill to its highest setting.
2 Melt the butter over a low heat, then remove from the heat and cool slightly. Mix in the egg yolks, mustard, beer and a dash each of Tabasco and Worcestershire sauces. Season well with salt and pepper, and fold in the cheese.
3 Place on the toast (either on its own or with sliced tomatoes or flat-leaf parsley leaves underneath), and grill until brown on the top.

James's tip

Egg yolks hold the rarebit mixture together, preventing it running off the toast when grilled. Alternatively, you can use about 2 tablespoons of breadcrumbs which act in the same way. If you feel the need, garnish with some chopped chives.

'Eat the rarebit on its own
or with some dressed salad leaves,
or simply cut it into small pieces
and eat as a canapé'

Crisp Potato Wedges with Mushy Peas and Balsamic Vinegar

Oil for deep-frying

1 x 600 g (1 lb 5 oz) tin
marrowfat peas,
drained and rinsed

25 g (1 oz) butter

2 large baking potatoes,
scrubbed

**Salt and freshly ground
black pepper**

2 tablespoons (approx)
balsamic vinegar

This idea comes from my father. When I was younger and we lived on a farm, he used to eat three portions of fish and chips on his own, and finish with a chip butty with mushy peas and balsamic vinegar. As you can gather, he's not really into dieting! I've just taken the idea and turned it into a snack.

1　Pre-heat the oil in a deep pan to a high heat.
2　Tip the peas into another pan with the butter and a touch of water. Bring to the boil, and simmer gently for about 5 minutes until the peas go mushy. Remove from the heat.
3　Using a knife, not a peeler, cut smallish rough wedges out of the potatoes, skin and all. Place them, in batches, in the pan of oil and fry until golden brown. Remove and place on some kitchen paper to get rid of any excess oil.
4　Mix some seasoning and balsamic vinegar into the peas, to taste, and serve in a bowl with the potato wedges around.

James's tip
Some supermarkets now sell ready-cooked potato skins for oven heating; handy if you don't fancy deep-frying.

Tzatziki

**150 g (5 ½ oz) natural
yoghurt**

¼ large cucumber,
finely diced

1 garlic clove,
peeled and chopped

**3 tablespoons chopped
fresh mint**

**Salt and freshly ground
black pepper**

A refreshing and healthy Greek dish that is usually served as a dip with pitta bread, but it can also be served as a garnish, or in conjunction with a main meal. It's virtually the same as an Indian *raita*, so is great with a curry.

Removing the seeds from the cucumber before dicing it prevents water seeping into the mixture and diluting the flavour.

1　Simply mix everything together in a bowl.
2　Serve immediately.

Tempura Squid with Pepperonella

650 g (1 lb 7 oz) prepared
squid (body only)

Oil for deep-frying

Batter

225 g (8 oz) plain flour

2 egg yolks

400 ml (14 fl oz) water

Salt and freshly ground
black pepper

To serve

2 x 15 g (½ oz) packets fresh
mint, chopped

1 x 200 g (7 oz) jar
Pepperonella (or some
roasted peppers,
see page 26)

This dish sounds more complicated than it actually is. Pepperonella, which is made with fresh tomatoes and freshly roasted peppers, can be bought ready made in jars. Using this saves a lot of hassle and time, and it tastes fine.

The squid must be cleaned and prepared properly; ask the fishmonger to do this. Squid should be cooked quickly on a high heat, only until golden brown, otherwise it will probably be tough.

1 Cut the squid across the body into rings.
2 Make the batter by mixing the flour, egg yolks and water together with a little salt and pepper. It should be quite thin. Don't worry if it's lumpy.
3 Heat the oil in a deep pan to a moderate to high heat. Dip the squid rings in the batter, then place in the hot oil and cook until golden brown: a few minutes only. Drain on some kitchen paper and season with a little salt.
4 Serve in a pile with chopped mint on the top and the Pepperonella on one side.

finger food

35

light meals

The dishes in this chapter are the sort I cook for myself when I'm at home: quick and easy, full of flavour, and hearty comfort food.

Flavour is all-important, of course, but timing must be considered too, because we're all on the move much of the time. Once again I've combined ready-prepared ingredients with fresh ones for maximum speed as well as maximum flavour.

Most of the recipes would serve two people (and I often eat enough for two, I must admit). Some are for four, because every now and again you want to share a meal when friends drop in unexpectedly and demand to be fed, or you invite some people over at the weekend.

Up north, where I come from, the term 'light meal' can be interpreted completely differently from down south. At home, a light lunch might consist of a bacon sandwich made from an entire breadstick, nearly a pound of bacon – fried not grilled – a couple of sliced large tomatoes and then the fat from the frying pan poured over it all! Even that is not as hearty as a traditional Sunday lunch – three courses of soup, meat and vegetables, and pudding. I usually fall asleep after that, which I haven't time for these days, so I now try to eat a little less for lunch.

However, one good thing about a roast is having left-overs, and I love things like cold beef or chicken. I have been known to cut off a thick slice of cold roast beef and pan-fry it with butter and onions – delicious with cold roast potatoes. But here I give you some ideas with left-overs that require very little additional cooking, if any at all.

There are a few new flavour combinations (some great ones for soup), and some perhaps unfamiliar flavours (truffle oil and duck fat, for instance). I've also introduced those store-cupboard stand-bys, pasta and rice, which, combined with pieces of fresh fish or chicken and the tang of a herb such as mint or coriander, can make a light lunch or supper dish that is out of this world. This is home cooking at its easiest and best.

Cream of Celeriac Soup with Truffle Oil

1 medium celeriac,
peeled and chopped

¼ leek,
cleaned and chopped

½ carrot,
scrubbed and chopped

½ white onion,
peeled and chopped

2 garlic cloves,
peeled and chopped

25 g (1 oz) butter

100 ml (3½ fl oz) white wine

**1 litre (1¾ pints) fresh
chicken stock**

200 ml (7 fl oz) double cream

**Salt and freshly ground
black pepper**

Truffle oil (see James's tip)

Serves 4

This was a dish created on the BBC's *Food and Drink* programme for a blind-date dance for 350 Durham students. It had to be an aphrodisiac meal, so I included some oysters. As these are very expensive, they're only optional. If using, remove from the shells, poach in a little champagne or sparkling wine for two minutes, then serve floating on top of the soup.

Celeriac is an under-used vegetable, although it's delicious and versatile. It can be puréed like potato, or puréed *with* potato; it's great flavoured with a vanilla pod and some curry powder; and it can also be blanched in small chips and served as a *rémoulade* salad – thin slices with mustard and mayonnaise – as a starter.

1 Prepare the vegetables first, just before cooking. Remember that the smaller you cut them, the quicker the soup will be made. (If you want to do this in advance, put the celeriac in water with a little lemon juice; otherwise it will turn brown.)

2 Put the butter, onion and garlic in a hot pan and cook for a few minutes, then add the celeriac, leek, carrot, white wine and stock. Bring to the boil and cook until the vegetables are soft: about 10–20 minutes.

3 Purée the vegetables and liquid with the cream in a food processor or blender until smooth. Season well and place in bowls. To finish, drizzle with a little truffle oil.

James's tip

Get someone rich to buy you some truffle oil. The best comes in a small square bottle, and is very expensive, but it is extremely potent (with a much more concentrated flavour than others). Just a little on this soup – or on a dish of pasta – is unequalled. To make truffle oil go a little further, mix it with some olive oil (not extra virgin): 100 ml (3½ fl oz) truffle oil mixed with 400 ml (14 fl oz) olive oil gives an oil that is still bursting with flavour.

Caesar Salad

4 garlic cloves, peeled

150 ml (5 fl oz) white wine

4 slices streaky bacon,
cut into lardons

2 slices white bread,
cut into chunky dice

25 g (1 oz) butter

2 cos lettuces

4 egg yolks

2 anchovy fillets

55 g (2 oz) Parmesan,
freshly grated

300 ml (10 fl oz) vegetable
oil

1 tablespoon Dijon mustard

Salt and freshly ground
black pepper

Serves 4

The basis of a good Caesar salad is the Parmesan. If you can get it, use Parmigiano Reggiano. Its superb flavour comes from the ageing process. While I was working in Italy I cooked with Parmesan that was six years old. Cheaper and younger *grana* cheeses, or Parmesans, are good none the less. But do not use the powdered stuff they call Parmesan, sold on the same shelf as the real McCoy. This is a foul travesty and should be banned.

The dressing for this salad is very special because the garlic is cooked in wine first; this gives it a delightfully subtle flavour.

And please, when making this salad, don't subject it to the common treatment of cutting everything into incredibly small pieces. Salad ingredients should be seen and not blended into obscurity.

1 Place the garlic in a pan with the wine, bring to the boil, and gently simmer for about 5 minutes until the cloves are soft.
2 Using two pans, crisp the bacon in one, without fat, and cook the bread in the butter in the other, until golden brown. Drain both on kitchen paper.
3 Remove the leaves from the lettuces, wash and dry well, then cut into chunky pieces.
4 Using a blender, mix the wine and garlic with the egg yolks, anchovy and cheese. Keep blending, adding the oil slowly to stop the mix from splitting. (This shouldn't happen as the cheese will make everything blend together more easily.) Then add the mustard, and season with salt and pepper to taste.
5 Throw all the ingredients into a bowl, mix together, and munch away.

One-minute Chilled Tomato Soup

6 plum tomatoes, quartered

2 garlic cloves, peeled and roughly chopped

¼ small red onion, peeled and roughly chopped

50 ml (2 fl oz) white wine

50 ml (2 fl oz) water

1 teaspoon tomato purée

5 ice cubes

1 x 15 g (½ oz) packet fresh basil leaves

Salt and freshly ground black pepper

Olive oil

To serve

French bread, warmed

Butter

Serves 4

A soup that really does take only a minute as the ice cubes chill it instantly.

I use plum tomatoes only if they are good ones: rich in colour and quite soft. But if you are unsure about the tomatoes' quality, use a 400 g (14 oz) tin of plum tomatoes, or fresh vine-ripened tomatoes which have a much stronger flavour and tend to be riper. Sugar can be added to a soup made with tinned tomatoes, which can be a little bitter.

For added flavour, use cubes of frozen stock. You could also garnish the soup with some olive-oil ice cubes: literally just olive oil frozen in ice-cube trays!

1 Put the tomatoes, garlic and onion in a food processor or blender. Then add the wine, water, tomato purée, ice cubes, fresh basil, lots of black pepper and a pinch of salt.

2 Place the lid on securely and blitz for about 30 seconds until all the ingredients are mixed together well. There may be some funny noises from the machine, but that's only the ice being ground up.

3 Remove and serve in chilled bowls, drizzled with a little olive oil, with some hot French bread and butter. You can garnish it further with some ripped-up fresh basil leaves.

Confit of Tomatoes on Toast

6 plum tomatoes

1 tablespoon fresh thyme
leaves

Rock salt and freshly
ground black pepper

4 garlic cloves,
peeled and chopped

Extra virgin olive oil

2 slices good Italian bread

Serves 2

I discovered this while working in a palazzo in northern Italy. It's one of the simplest dishes, yet tastes like one of the best, and I lived on it at breakfast time. The mother of the household would cook a half crate of tomatoes at a time in a lovely old tray that had been blackened with many years of use. She used about 2 litres of local olive oil at a time and saved any left-over oil for the following day.

1 Pre-heat the oven to 220°C/425°F/gas mark 7. Place the tomatoes in a small ovenproof dish and sprinkle with the thyme and rock salt. Add the garlic, season with pepper, and fill the dish with olive oil, a quarter way up the tomatoes. Bake in the oven for 8–10 minutes.

2 Drizzle the bread with olive oil and rock salt, and toast it under the grill or in a griddle pan (see page 142). Spoon the tomatoes on to the bread, with plenty of olive oil.

Sautéed Potatoes with Garlic, Thyme and Duck Fat

450 g (1 lb) new potatoes,
scrubbed and dried

100 ml (3½ fl oz) duck fat

2 sprigs of fresh thyme

½ whole garlic bulb

Salt and freshly ground
black pepper

French bread (optional)

Serves 2

Potatoes and duck fat are a great combination and this is a dish after my own heart: I was brought up on bread and dripping, just as the French are brought up on goose or duck fat. Duck fat is sold just like butter in France, but you can find it outside France in good delicatessens in tins and jars. Rosemary can be used instead of thyme.

1 Cut the potatoes in half and place in a heavy frying pan with the duck fat and fresh thyme.

2 Cut the garlic in half, skin and all. Add this to the pan, and cook the whole thing gently over a moderate heat for about 15–20 minutes until the potatoes are golden brown.

3 Season the potatoes with salt and pepper and serve them plus their fat in a bowl, alone, or with some French bread. For the health-conscious, drain off and save the flavoured duck fat for another use.

Tinned Tomato and Pesto Risotto

2 x 800 g (1 lb 12 oz) tins
plum tomatoes

½ red onion,
peeled and finely diced

3 garlic cloves,
peeled and finely diced

25 g (1 oz) butter

250 g (9 oz) risotto rice,
such as *arborio*

115 g (4 oz) piece Parmesan

Salt and freshly ground
black pepper

2 tablespoons pesto sauce

2 x 15 g (½ oz) packets
fresh basil

Olive oil

Serves 4

Tinned tomatoes are better than fresh for this risotto as they have a superior flavour once they are puréed. The colour is better too: bright red, rather than the pink of fresh tomatoes.

Use a proper risotto rice, such as *arborio* or, better still, *carnaroli* which soaks up the liquid more. Never buy those coloured rices on offer in supermarkets. They're just a gimmick, and don't really taste of anything once they are cooked.

1 Place the tomatoes and their juices in a blender, and purée until smooth. Leave to one side.

2 Sauté the onion and garlic in the butter for a minute.

3 Add the rice to the onion, and continue cooking for a further minute, before adding three-quarters of the puréed tomato. Bring to the boil and gently simmer for about 15 minutes, stirring continuously to stop it burning. If the mix is getting too dry, add some of the remaining puréed tomato liquid.

4 Using a potato peeler, shave about a quarter of the Parmesan into shavings. Then grate the remainder.

5 Add the grated cheese to the rice along with some salt, lots of black pepper (which brings out the flavour of the tomato) and the pesto. Stir well. To finish, add the fresh basil leaves, just ripped up and mixed in.

6 Spoon into soup plates and garnish with the shavings of Parmesan and a drizzle of olive oil.

James's tip

Be careful when adding the tomato liquid to the rice. Because it's thicker than a traditional stock, you have to stir almost all the time to prevent the rice sticking and burning on the bottom of the pan. And don't add all the liquid at the same time because eventually the risotto could become too wet.

Grilled Goat's Cheese with a Broad Bean, Pancetta and Mint Salad

2 slices of Italian white bread (*ciabatta* or *foccaccia*)

Olive oil

Rock salt and freshly ground black pepper

125 g (4½ oz) *pancetta*, diced

1 garlic clove, peeled and diced

¼ red onion, peeled and diced

3 tablespoons balsamic vinegar

1 x 100 g (3½ oz) piece goat's cheese (see James's tips), cut in half

225 g (8 oz) frozen broad beans, defrosted and peeled (see James's tips)

1 tablespoon pesto sauce

2 tablespoons chopped fresh mint

2 x 15 g (½ oz) packets fresh basil

Serves 2

Pancetta is an Italian cured and rolled belly pork, which is much tastier than the British type of bacon. It contains plenty of fat so is ideal for cooking with other ingredients. Don't add any extra fat to the pan as it is the fat being rendered – the fat coming out of the *pancetta* – that crisps the meat. You can buy *pancetta* in Italian delicatessens, or diced, in vacuum packs, in supermarkets.

1. Pre-heat the oven to 200°C/400°F/gas mark 6. Place the slices of bread on an ovenproof tray, drizzle with olive oil, sprinkle with rock salt, and bake in the oven for about 5 minutes until crisp but not coloured.
2. In a hot pan, cook the *pancetta* without any added fat until crisp and golden brown. Then add the garlic, onion and vinegar, and cook together for a minute. Remove from the heat.
3. Pre-heat the grill. Put the goat's cheese on the bread, season with salt and pepper, and drizzle with olive oil. Place under the grill until golden brown.
4. Add the peeled beans, pesto and mint to the bacon mix. Stir well and season to taste. Place the bean mix on two plates, top with the goat's cheese and bread and drizzle with olive oil.

James's tips

Goat's cheese has a sharp taste that goes well with broad beans. Try to get young Sainte-Maure or Crottin de Chavignol, or a milder British Gedi. More mature goat's cheeses tend to be crumbly, with a concentrated chalky flavour which some people find off-putting.

To reveal the attractive bright green interior of broad beans (frozen or fresh) blanch them in boiling water for about half a minute, then drain. Cover with cold water to stop the cooking, and drain again. Peel off the outer skin. This dish definitely works better with frozen beans than with fresh.

'A dish that can be
rustled up in a couple of minutes
from just a few supermarket
ingredients, which looks and
tastes fantastic'

Wafer-thin Tomato, Emmenthal and Grain Mustard Tart

150 g (5½ oz) filo pastry

Olive oil

3 tablespoons grain mustard

55 g (2 oz) Emmenthal cheese, sliced

6 tomatoes, sliced

Salt and freshly ground black pepper

To serve

2 tablespoons balsamic vinegar

5 tablespoons olive oil

100 g (3½ oz) rocket or baby spinach leaves

A little basil pesto

Serves 2

This tart is superb served hot with a dressed salad of spinach or rocket. You can also use other toppings which are suggested below.

I'm a great believer in saving time in cooking and, as I've said, ready-prepared filo and puff pastries are great products for quick and tasty cooking. Both are actually better bought fresh (in delicatessens, ethnic shops and some supermarkets). Frozen filo tends to flake a bit in preparation, unless you cover it with a damp tea-towel, and use melted butter instead of olive oil.

1 If using frozen pastry, allow it to defrost. Pre-heat the oven to 230°C/450°F/gas mark 8. Lay a sheet of pastry on a baking sheet, brush it with a little olive oil, then put another sheet on top. Keep adding sheets in this way.

2 When you have built up about 12–15 layers of pastry, spread the top with the mustard and lay the cheese over it. Place the tomato slices all over the top of the tart, overlapping them as you go.

3 Season well, drizzle with olive oil and bake in the oven for 15 minutes until the pastry base is cooked. Remove from the oven.

4 In a bowl mix the balsamic vinegar with the olive oil and some salt and pepper. Combine the salad leaves with the dressing.

5 Remove the tart from the tray and drizzle with the pesto. Serve with the dressed salad.

James's tip

There are a number of alternative toppings. Why not try smoked salmon, red onion and crème fraîche; wild mushrooms, thyme and Mozzarella cheese; figs and Gorgonzola cheese; or spinach, crème fraîche and shelled mussels.

Pasta with Pesto

400 g (14 oz) dried penne

Salt and freshly ground black pepper

85 g (3 oz) Parmesan, made into shavings

Basil pesto

55 g (2 oz) fresh basil

1 garlic clove, peeled

2 anchovy fillets

1 tablespoon pine kernels, toasted

6 tablespoons olive oil

25 g (1 oz) Parmesan, grated

Serves 4

I don't normally suggest making pesto, but with a bought brand of pesto this dish is like fish and chips without the newspaper: it just doesn't taste the same.

1 Cook the penne In a generous amount of boiling salted water, usually about 10–12 minutes.

2 Meanwhile, place the basil, garlic, anchovy, pine kernels, olive oil and grated cheese in a blender. Purée the mix and season with salt and pepper. Add more oil if necessary – enough to create a thickish purée.

3 Drain the pasta well and place in a bowl with some ground black pepper and salt. Mix the pesto through it. Place in a bowl and put the Parmesan shavings on top.

Pasta with Chorizo Sausage, Tomato and Rocket

1 very small *chorizo* sausage, thinly sliced

2 garlic cloves, peeled and chopped

Olive oil

1 x 600 g (1 lb 5 oz) tin plum tomatoes

200 g (7 oz) dried penne

55 g (2 oz) rocket leaves

1 x 20 g (¾ oz) packet fresh flat-leaf parsley, chopped

1 x 150 g (5½ oz) ball buffalo Mozzarella, grated

Salt and freshly ground black pepper

Serves 2

There are fashions in food, and *chorizo* is the Armani of the moment. A spicy dried pork sausage, it looks like a little salami. It needs infusing first, to bring out the full flavour, and shouldn't really be eaten raw. Some supermarkets and delicatessens, however, are offering a larger *piccante* version, usually sold thinly sliced.

1 In a pan heat up a few tablespoons of olive oil, add the *chorizo* and garlic, and cook for a few minutes. Add the tomatoes, bring to the boil, and cook for about 10 minutes.

2 Cook the pasta in a generous amount of boiling salted water following the timing given on the packet, usually about 10–12 minutes. Drain well.

3 Rip the rocket leaves in half and add to the sauce together with three-quarters of the parsley. Season well. Mix the sauce and pasta together and place in a dish. Top with the grated Mozzarella and the rest of the parsley, and serve.

Linguine with Roast Figs and Herbs

4 large fresh figs

8 slices of speck bacon
(or *prosciutto* or Parma ham)

2 shallots,
peeled and chopped

2 garlic cloves,
peeled and chopped

Olive oil

100 ml (3½ fl oz) white wine

200 g (7 oz) Dolcelatte
cheese

300 ml (10 fl oz) double
cream

Salt and freshly ground
black pepper

2 large sprigs fresh mint,
chopped

1 x 15 g (½ oz) packet fresh
basil, chopped

1 x 15 g (½ oz) packet fresh
chives, chopped

40 g (1½ oz) Parmesan
cheese, in shavings

400 g (14 oz) linguine

Serves 4

It has been fashionable recently to make your own pasta, supposedly like the Italians themselves. But anyone who has worked in good Italian kitchens knows that a lot of them use good-quality dried pastas, not the fresh variety.

The mixture of textures and flavours here is unusual, and very sexy. You could add toasted walnuts, almonds, pistachios or pine kernels for additional texture and sex appeal. This dish should only be made with fresh figs, not tinned or dried.

1 Pre-heat the oven to 230°C/450°F/gas mark 8. Wrap the figs in the speck bacon and secure with wooden cocktail sticks. Bake in the oven for about 5–6 minutes, until the bacon is nice and crisp.

2 Meanwhile, sweat the shallots and garlic in 1 tablespoon of olive oil for a few minutes, then add the white wine. Boil to reduce by half, then add the cheese and cream. Reduce until slightly thickened, but do not boil, or the mixture will split because of the fat in the cheese. Season with salt and pepper and add some of the herbs.

3 Cook the pasta in a generous amount of boiling salted water, with a little oil in it, following the timing given on the packet, usually about 6-8 minutes.

4 Remove the cocktail sticks from the figs. Combine the pasta and sauce, divide between plates, and garnish with the figs and the remaining fresh herbs. Top with the shavings of Parmesan.

light meals

49

Cod with Cumin and Coriander Lentils

½ **carrot,**
scrubbed and finely diced

¼ **leek,**
cleaned and finely diced

¼ **red onion,**
peeled and finely diced

25 g (1 oz) **butter**

150 ml (5 fl oz) **red wine**

1 x 400 g (14 oz) **tin lentils,**
drained and rinsed

2 x 225 g (8 oz) **thick pieces
cod,** skin on

½ teaspoon **balsamic vinegar**

1 level teaspoon **ground
cumin**

**Salt and freshly ground
black pepper**

1 x 15 g (½ oz) **packet fresh
coriander,** roughly chopped

Serves 2

Puy lentils, small and grey-green in colour, are grown in France. With a very distinctive flavour, they keep their shape and colour when cooked. They are available tinned as well as dry, which here speeds the whole thing up considerably. Although any type of lentil will do for this recipe, *lentilles de Puy* really are the best. These flavoured lentils go really well with seared scallops and chicken as well as with the cod here.

1 Sauté the carrot, leek and onion in a pan in half the butter until softened. Then add the red wine and drained lentils. Warm through gently while you cook the cod.

2 In a non-stick pan, place the cod, skin side down, in the remaining butter and sauté for about 2–3 minutes. Turn over, and cook for a further 2 minutes. Try to avoid turning it more than once, as cod will fall to bits very easily if it is fresh.

3 Season the lentils with the vinegar, ground cumin, salt and pepper, then fold in the fresh chopped coriander.

4 Serve the lentils in a bowl with the cod on the top, and a glass of wine.

James's tip

Buy the best quality, freshest cod. It should be pure white in colour, and it shouldn't smell of anything, not even of fish. To hold the fish together, as its flesh is very flaky, get it cut at least 2.5 cm (1 in) thick, and keep the skin on. The skin crisps up in the cooking and adds considerably to the flavour.

Deep-fried Salmon Belly in Beer Batter

450 g (1 lb) salmon belly,
cut into strips

Oil for deep-frying

Tzatziki (see page 34)

Batter

225 g (8 oz) self-raising flour

2 tablespoons chopped
fresh mint

Salt and freshly ground
black pepper

20 g (¾ oz) sesame seeds

350 ml (12 fl oz) ale or lager

Serves 2

This recipe uses the salmon belly flaps many good fishmongers sell for next to nothing, or even give away. These are the bits of the salmon which are normally cleaned off and discarded after filleting. They are full of flavour, but keep the skin on as this helps everything hold together during the cooking.

1 Heat the oil in a deep pan to a high heat, or use a deep-fat fryer.
2 Place the flour in a bowl. Add the mint, salt and pepper and sesame seeds, and slowly mix in the beer. Don't worry about lumps; just make it into a thick consistency.
3 Mix the salmon strips into the batter. Place them, once coated, into the hot fat one by one to stop them from sticking to each other (keep shaking the basket to stop them sticking on the bottom). Cook them in two batches to speed up the cooking time.
4 Once they are golden brown, remove the salmon strips and place on kitchen paper to drain off any excess oil.
5 Pile them up in a bowl or on a plate, put the yoghurt and cucumber dip in a separate bowl. Dip and eat.

Seared Salmon with Lime, Coriander and Tomato Salsa

2 x 175 g (6 oz) fillets salmon
(skin on, but no bones)

**Salt and freshly ground
black pepper**

1 tablespoon olive oil

Salsa

1 red pepper

6 tomatoes

1 small red onion, peeled

½ fresh red chilli,
de-seeded (see page 137)

**1 x 15 g (½ oz) packet fresh
coriander**, chopped

Juice and zest of 2 limes

Serves 2

As flavour is the most important aim in cooking, why do so many of us, chefs included, throw away half of the food in preparation – the skins of apples, for instance – which hold so much flavour? Skinning, coring and de-seeding tomatoes should be banned as well. Use the whole thing; don't mess around with food.

1 Cut the pepper in half, remove the seeds and stalk, and cut the flesh into small dice. Chop the tomatoes into small dice, together with the red onion and chilli. Mix with the pepper dice.

2 Season the salmon and cook in the oil, skin side down, only turning once to stop it from breaking up. This should take no longer than 5–7 minutes.

3 Mix the chopped coriander and lime zest and juice into the pepper and tomato. Season well.

4 Place the salmon on the plate with the salsa to one side.

'What could be tastier than crisp-skinned salmon served with a salsa that sings with the flavours of lime and coriander...'

supper parties

The next best thing to indulging myself on a quiet evening at home is cooking for those who are closest to me, friends I enjoy spending time with. But why does it always have to be me who does the cooking? I think I've only been asked out to supper three times by friends since leaving college, and on one of those occasions I ended up cooking a meal for twenty and spending the whole evening in the kitchen. I'd passed on my recipe for Coq au Vin at a friend's request, but hadn't realized she expected me to cook it as well. At least if you cook, you don't have to wash up – well, that's *my* rule.

Some of the recipes I've included here have come from my family: from my grandmother, my mother and my father. Some of my granny's recipes are over a hundred years old. In fact, this chapter more than others reflects my experiences: nineteen years of growing up on the farm, and my travels in France and Italy. It was there that I really learned what traditional food and cooking should be all about: going out to the market, choosing, sniffing, feeling, buying, and then taking it home to prepare immediately, or to kill, gut and pluck – the whole process.

Once again, the recipes are quick and simple, but more hearty and filling; they include a few more expensive ingredients, but these are still married with cheaper ones to keep the overall costs down. The most important thing is that they taste good and look impressive – all that you need when entertaining. The desserts, particularly, include a number of 'cheating' and corner-cutting ideas. These involve bought, ready-prepared ingredients available from most supermarkets, but once you've been creative with them, they look spectacular.

There are ideas for all three courses, and don't forget that you could offer a selection of finger foods as a starter if you liked. A few menu suggestions which might inspire you can be found on the next page.

Suggested menus

One-hour menu

A quick and simple menu that can be cooked in (actually less than) an hour.

Rustic Tomato, Bread and Basil Soup (page 66)

Roast Cod with Smoked Garlic and Vanilla Mash (page 73)

Baked Bananas with Rosemary, Toffee Sauce and Vanilla Ice-cream (page 81)

Quick two-course menu

Two dishes that are enough to fill you up and impress your friends.

Paillard of Chicken with Mozzarella, Prosciutto and Sage (page 76)

Pineapple and Black Pepper Tarte Tatin (page 85)

Hearty menu

This would have to be my granny's choice, as it's all her food. It's definitely a menu for winter (or if you haven't eaten for two days).

Granny's Yorkshire Pudding with Onions (page 70)

Ham, Potato, Leek and Herb Hotpot (page 78)

Steamed Sponge Pudding with Tarragon Apples (page 87)

My favourite menu

What can I say? The risotto reminds me of Italy, the pheasant of Yorkshire, and the brûlée of France.

Crevette, Asparagus and Red Pepper Risotto (page 68)

Mother's Pheasant with Wild Garlic Leaves, Shallots and Bacon (page 74)

Vanilla Crème Brûlée (page 83)

STARTERS

My interpretation of a starter is a small collection of flavours married together, which whets the appetite, but doesn't satisfy it. As always, because time is of the essence, many of these starters can be prepared in advance.

Chorizo, Butter Bean and Truffle Oil Soup

1 very small *chorizo* sausage, sliced

½ small onion, peeled and chopped

2 garlic cloves, peeled and chopped

1 tablespoon olive oil

2 x 400 g (14 oz) tins butter beans

200 ml (7 fl oz) white wine

500 ml (18 fl oz) fresh chicken stock

2 sprigs each fresh thyme and parsley

200 ml (7 fl oz) double cream

Salt and freshly ground black pepper

Truffle oil (see page 38)

To serve
French or Italian bread

Serves 4

You don't need to worry about using dried butter beans for this soup, as the tinned ones are perfect. The soup is good enough just made with beans and finished off with truffle oil, but the addition of the *chorizo* gives it an extra spicy kick.

1 Place the *chorizo*, onion and garlic in a hot pan with the oil and sauté slowly for a few minutes until the *chorizo* softens slightly.

2 Drain the beans, rinse and drain again, then add to the pan with the wine and stock. Bring to the boil, add the thyme and parsley, and simmer for about 10 minutes.

3 Using a blender, purée the soup until all of the lumps have gone.

4 Add the cream and seasoning, heat through a little, then place in soup bowls. Finish with a drizzle of truffle oil. Serve with some chunky pieces of bread.

A Warm Salad of New Potatoes, Raclette Cheese and Red Pepper

1 red pepper

Olive oil

3 tablespoons balsamic vinegar

Salt and freshly ground black pepper

225 g (8 oz) cooked new potatoes

3 tablespoons grain mustard

1 sprig fresh rosemary, chopped

85 g (3 oz) Raclette (or Gruyère) cheese, grated

½ head *frisée* lettuce

60 g (2¼ oz) *tapenade*

4 sprigs fresh basil

Serves 4

Whenever you have any left-over new potatoes, this is what you could do instead of simply frying them in butter: make a meal of them. This is great as a starter with a glass of Chardonnay, but could make a filling lunch dish as well.

Here I suggest bought *tapenade* made with olives, but if you don't like olives (like me), use the sun-dried tomato *tapenade* on page 29.

1 Pre-heat the oven to 200°C/400°F/gas mark 6. Cut the red pepper in half, remove the seeds and stalk, and place, cut side down, on an oven tray. Drizzle with olive oil and bake in the oven until the skin is brown, about 15–20 minutes. Remove from the oven, place in a bowl, cover with clingfilm while hot, and leave to cool down. Peel the skin off the pepper and cut the flesh into small dice.

2 Mix the pepper dice with 6 tablespoons of the olive oil, the vinegar and some seasoning to make the dressing.

3 Dice the cooked potatoes, skin and all, and put in a bowl with the mustard, seasoning and the chopped fresh rosemary. Place in a microwave for about 30 seconds to warm up and then press into four 5 cm (2 in) stainless-steel rings on a baking tray. Top with the grated cheese. (At this stage, if you haven't got a microwave, put into the still warm oven, or a low oven, to soften the cheese and heat the potatoes through.) Place under a pre-heated hot grill to brown the top.

4 Place a small pile of *frisée* leaves in the middle of each plate, and the ring of potato and cheese on the top. Lift the steel ring off, leaving the moulded shape on the leaves, cheese on the top. Spoon a mound of the tapenade on top of the cheese.

5 Chop the fresh basil and add to the red pepper dressing. Check for seasoning again. Spoon round the edges of the plates and serve.

Grilled Sardines with a Raw Vegetable Salsa

12 fresh medium sardines, cleaned

½ small carrot, peeled and finely chopped

½ red onion, peeled and finely chopped

1 red pepper, de-seeded and finely chopped

½ fresh red chilli, de-seeded and finely chopped (see page 137)

1 garlic clove, peeled and finely chopped

¼ small cucumber, finely chopped

Salt and freshly ground black pepper

Olive oil

Juice and zest of 2 lemons

1 x 15 g (½ oz) packet fresh chives, chopped

1 x 15 g (½ oz) packet fresh coriander, chopped

Serves 4

Sardines are very underrated, but fresh sardines (and anchovies) are superb, not a bit like tinned ones. Ask your fishmonger to gut and scale the fish and to remove the heads if you're put off by gleaming eyes staring at you. It also saves you a lot of time and mess.

1 Prepare the vegetable dice and mix them all together, apart from the cucumber.

2 Put the sardines on a tray, season them and drizzle with olive oil. Place under a hot pre-heated grill and cook for 3 minutes on one side. Turn them over and cook on the other side for another 2–3 minutes. Make sure the skin is good and crisp, as sardines are like mackerel: the skin must be crisp for maximum taste.

3 Add the cucumber dice and the juice and zest of the lemons to the diced vegetables, together with 2 tablespoons of olive oil and some seasoning. Place the mix in a pan and just warm through, or sling it in a microwave for a few seconds to warm it up. Don't overheat or the cucumber will go to mush.

4 Add the chopped herbs to the salsa, spoon over the hot sardines and serve.

'This is a dish I invented at home some time ago. It came about through a mistake I made while cooking. If most chefs are honest, that is how a lot of new dishes are created'

Rustic Tomato, Bread and Basil Soup

1 red onion, peeled and diced

6 garlic cloves, peeled and diced

Olive oil

300 ml (10 fl oz) white wine

150 ml (5 fl oz) water

12 plum tomatoes, quartered

1 x 800 g (1 lb 12 oz) tin plum tomatoes

Salt and freshly ground black pepper

½ loaf *ciabatta*

1 x 15 g (½ oz) packet fresh basil

Serves 4

Bread is used throughout Europe to thicken soups, whereas we in Britain tend to use flour or potato. I've used two types of tomato here: the fresh tomatoes to give texture and tinned tomatoes to give colour and flavour. Please don't try to purée this soup when it's ready. It's meant to be rustic and chunky in look and texture – good wholesome food. This is a very easy soup: the whole thing can be made from start to finish in about five minutes.

1 Heat about 3 tablespoons of olive oil in a pan and cook the onion and garlic for a few minutes to soften them slightly.
2 Add the wine, water and all the tomatoes. Cover with a lid, bring to the boil and season with salt and lots of pepper.
3 Dice the bread and stir it into the soup, along with the freshly ripped basil leaves. Place in a bowl, and drizzle with olive oil on the top.

'Flavour should amount to 75 per cent of a finished dish; people will remember it because it tasted good, not because it looked pretty'

Char-grilled Smoked Salmon with Rocket and Parmesan

55 g (2 oz) piece fresh
Parmesan

Olive oil

2 tablespoons balsamic
vinegar

Salt and freshly ground
black pepper

200 g (7 oz) rocket leaves

225 g (8 oz) sliced smoked
salmon

Serves 4

Smoked salmon on its own is superb, but as when added to scrambled eggs, cooked smoked salmon is divine. Here I've taken an unusual approach and char-grilled it in a griddle pan (see page 142), which gives it great flavour.

This dish could also be served as a light main course for two people.

1   Using a speed potato peeler (see page 142), shave all the cheese into thin strips, and set to one side.
2   Mix 4 tablespoons of the olive oil and the vinegar together with some seasoning. Mix into the rocket leaves quickly and carefully, and place on the plates.
3   Heat a griddle pan to a high heat. Remove the salmon from the packet, fold each slice into three to make one thicker slice. Season with black pepper and drizzle on one side with a little olive oil.
4   When the pan is very hot, place the salmon on it, oiled side down, and leave for about 15 seconds. Turn it 90 degrees, cook for another 15 seconds, then remove. Do not turn it over; only cook on one side.
5   Sprinkle the rocket with the Parmesan shavings and place the salmon, charred side up, on the top. Serve immediately, ideally with a glass of chilled Chardonnay.

Crevette, Asparagus and Red Pepper Risotto

½ **red onion,**
peeled and finely chopped

2 **garlic cloves,**
peeled and finely chopped

2 tablespoons olive oil

250 g (9 oz) *arborio* **rice**

**600 ml (1 pint) fresh fish
stock**

1 **red pepper,** de-seeded and
cut into large cubes

8 asparagus spears, trimmed

10 large cooked crevettes,
peeled

**100 ml (3½ fl oz) double
cream**

85 g (3 oz) Parmesan,
freshly grated

**Salt and freshly ground
black pepper**

**1 x 15 g (½ oz) packet fresh
basil**

a few shavings of Parmesan
(optional)

Serves 4

Crevettes have a wonderful flavour and are available from good fishmongers but if you can't find them, use fresh prawns instead. Asparagus is now available all year round and although nothing is as good as the new English variety, imported asparagus is acceptable. It's important that everything is added separately and at the appropriate time, as it is all very easy to over-cook.

1 Using a large pan, cook the onion and garlic in the oil until they soften slightly.

2 Add the rice and cook for about 30 seconds, stirring, then add the stock and bring to the boil. Simmer for about 15 minutes until the rice is cooked and has a porridge-like consistency. Keep stirring to avoid it sticking to the bottom of the pan. Stir the red pepper cubes into the rice about halfway through the cooking.

3 Meanwhile, cut the asparagus spears in half across. Place in boiling water and cook for a few minutes until just cooked but not soft. Drain well.

4 When the rice is cooked, add the crevettes, cream and grated Parmesan. Chop up the asparagus bottoms (not the tips) and mix them in as well. Season with salt and pepper and finish with the ripped-up fresh basil leaves.

5 Place the risotto into bowls, and garnish with the asparagus tips and Parmesan shavings (if using).

Granny's Yorkshire Pudding with Onions

225 g (8 oz) plain flour

**Salt and freshly ground
black pepper**

8 eggs

600 ml (1 pint) milk

55 g (2 oz) good dripping

Onions

**2 white onions,
peeled and sliced**

250 ml (9 fl oz) red wine

**400 ml (14 fl oz) fresh
beef stock**

Serves 4

Granny knows best, especially when making Yorkshire puddings. However there are some golden rules to follow: you must cook on a high heat first, then turn the oven down; and you mustn't open the oven door at all for the first 20–25 minutes. And for the most successful results, make your mixture a day in advance and leave it to rest in the fridge.

1 Place the flour and some seasoning into a bowl. Add the eggs, mixing in with a whisk, and then the milk, mixing slowly to prevent lumps forming. At this point, put the bowl in the fridge overnight covered with some clingfilm.

2 Pre-heat the oven to 220°C/425°F/gas mark 7. Take four non-stick Yorkshire pudding tins (about 13 cm/5 in in diameter). Put a little of the dripping in each of the tins, but don't use it all. Put the tins into the hot oven. Before you add the mix to the tins, the fat in the tins should be smoking hot.

3 As you pour in the mix, so that it fills the tins to the top, the mix should seal on the edges. Working fast, place them back in the oven, close the door and leave it closed for about 20–25 minutes.

4 Meanwhile, cook the onions in a pan in the remaining dripping, for about 10 minutes, then add the wine and stock. Reduce until you have a nice thickened mixture: about another 10 minutes or so. Season well.

5 Turn the oven down to 190°C/375°F/gas mark 5 and cook the Yorkshires for a further 10 minutes to set the bottom of the puds thoroughly. Remove from the oven, place on plates, and serve the thick onion gravy in the middle.

'Some of my granny's recipes are over 100 years old, and have been passed down through the Yorkshire generations'

Mother's Pheasant with Wild Garlic Leaves, Shallots and Bacon

2 large pheasants, oven-ready

1 carrot

½ leek

1 onion, peeled

400 ml (14 fl oz) red wine

1 litre (1¾ pints) fresh chicken stock

4 sprigs fresh thyme

Salt and freshly ground black pepper

1 tablespoon olive oil

16 rashers streaky bacon

16 shallots, peeled

40 g (1½ oz) butter

8 handfuls freshly picked wild garlic leaves

Serves 4

The best dish I have ever had. It uses only ingredients from my home in Yorkshire: local pheasant, shallots from the garden, garlic leaves from the woods, and bacon from our pigs.

I can't tell you where to get wild garlic, as I only know one place in Yorkshire where it grows, but it's found in damp woods and shady lanes; it has white flowers and dark green leaves which are like a cross between dock and dandelion. It's the smell that will alert you: it is profoundly garlicky. It's really worth making the effort to find it, but if not possible, try using 450 g (1 lb) spinach with two cloves of garlic.

1 Remove the breasts and legs from the pheasant and leave to one side.

2 Pre-heat the oven to 220°C/425°F/gas mark 7. For the sauce, dice the carrot, leek and three-quarters of the onion and place this and the pheasant carcasses in a roasting tray. Roast in the oven for about 1 hour until nice and brown. Leave the oven on.

3 Remove from the oven and place in a large pan with the red wine, stock and half the fresh thyme. Bring to the boil and simmer gently without a lid so the liquor can reduce.

4 Season the pheasant legs and breasts with salt and pepper and seal in a hot pan in the olive oil. Put in an ovenproof dish in one layer and cover with the bacon. Add the shallots and remaining thyme to the dish. Place in the oven at the same heat, and roast for about 15 minutes.

5 Meanwhile, finely dice the remaining onion and cook in half the butter in a pan over a high heat for a few minutes. Throw in the garlic leaves and cook for about 1 minute only, until wilted. Remove from the heat.

6 Strain the sauce and continue to reduce over a high heat.

7 Remove the pheasant from the oven and leave to stand for about 5–10 minutes to rest. Add the remaining butter and some seasoning to the sauce.

8 Season the garlic leaves, place on the plates and put the pheasant on the top with the bacon, shallots and thyme from the pan. Pour over the sauce and serve.

Paillard of Chicken with Mozzarella, Prosciutto and Sage

4 x 225 g (8 oz) chicken breasts (no bone)

Salt and freshly ground black pepper

Olive oil

12 sage leaves

8 tablespoons plum chutney (see page 94)

2 x 150 g (5½ oz) balls buffalo Mozzarella cheese

8 slices *prosciutto*

8 sprigs fresh basil

Serves 4

The combination of chicken, Mozzarella, plum and sage here is really successful, and the whole lot is like one big, tall, messy pizza. Trendy chefs are even using thin slices of salmon as a base for different pizza-style toppings. Whatever next?

1 Cut the chicken breasts in half, but not all the way through, just enough to open the breasts out flat (called butterflying). Season the chicken well, and cook in a hot sauté pan in 4 tablespoons of the olive oil, colouring both sides well: about 8–10 minutes altogether.

2 When they are cooked, place 3 sage leaves on the top of each breast, along with 2 tablespoons of plum chutney.

3 Remove the Mozzarella from the packets and drain. Chop into dice. Divide the cheese into four piles, and place a pile on each butterflied chicken. Finish with the slices of *prosciutto*. Drizzle with olive oil and season well.

4 Place under a pre-heated hot grill to crisp the bacon. It should take only a few minutes. This will also melt the cheese.

5 Place the chicken on plates and pour the juices remaining in the pan over the top. Garnish with the fresh basil.

'People make the mistake of thinking truffles, *foie gras* and oysters are the best food. But *all* food is potentially delicious and packed with flavour'

Grilled Pork with a Spicy Borlotti Bean, Pancetta and Cabbage Stew

225 g (8 oz) *pancetta*, diced

½ red onion, peeled and finely chopped

4 garlic cloves, peeled and finely chopped

½ small carrot, scrubbed and finely chopped

4 x 200 g (7 oz) pork chops

Salt and freshly ground black pepper

1 x 400 g (14 oz) tin *borlotti* **beans,** drained and rinsed

500 ml (18 fl oz) fresh chicken stock

1 fresh green chilli, de-seeded and finely diced

8 fresh Savoy cabbage leaves

1 x 20 g (¾ oz) packet flat-leaf parsley, chopped

Serves 4

Good roast pork with crunchy crackling is one of the joys of eating. When I was about eight, I used to nick the crackling from under the grill while father was watching television, and eat it with some rock salt at the back door (for a quick exit).

1 First, sauté the *pancetta* in a pan without any oil (there is enough fat in it already). Once the *pancetta* is crisp, add the onion, garlic and carrot to the pan and cook for about one minute.

2 Season the pork chops well and place under a pre-heated hot grill for about 12 minutes altogether, turning them over every few minutes. When the pork is cooked, the fat should be a nice brown colour.

3 While the pork is cooking, add the beans, chicken stock and finely diced chilli to the onion mix and bring to the boil. Cook for about 5 minutes.

4 Thinly slice the cabbage leaves, add to the stew, and cook for about a further 2 minutes.

5 Remove the chops from the grill and finish the stew with lots of fresh chopped parsley. Pour the stew into four large bowls, place the chops on the top and serve.

Ham, Potato, Leek and Herb Hotpot

1 red onion,
peeled and finely chopped

4 garlic cloves,
peeled and finely chopped

2 small leeks,
cleaned and sliced

225 g (8 oz) butter

200 ml (7 fl oz) white wine

**500 ml (18 fl oz) fresh ham
stock**

450 g (1 lb) new potatoes,
cooked

550 g (1¼ lb) cooked ham,
cut into chunks

**Salt and freshly ground
black pepper**

**65 g (2½ oz) each of
chopped fresh basil, parsley,
chives and coriander**

French bread (optional)

Serves 4

This is adapted from my grandmother's recipe. For the stock, she used the end knuckle of hams left over from the butcher's slicer, and for the meat, the bits around the bones of a carved joint. Whatever you use, the ham must be good quality, not a sliced, processed ham bought in a packet.

I use a great deal of herbs because the hotpot should be like a thick stew. As the sauce mainly consists of butter, the herbs serve to thicken and flavour it.

1 Using about 55 g (2 oz) of the butter, sauté the onion, garlic and leeks in a large pan, until soft.
2 Add the white wine, ham stock, potatoes and ham and cook for 5–10 minutes until everything is nice and hot.
3 Drain off the liquid, keeping the meat and vegetables warm. Gently simmer the liquid, adding the remaining butter bit by bit, whisking all the time to thicken the sauce. Do not boil.
4 Put all the ingredients back into the sauce and season. To finish, add all the chopped fresh herbs. Serve piping hot in bowls with some French bread.

James's tip

If you don't have the time or the inclination to make ham stock yourself, use fresh chicken stock, available in tubs from supermarkets.

'Giving supper parties is very much my style, with a relaxed atmosphere – me in the kitchen, and people milling around watching me cook'

dinners for two

By their very nature, dinners for two must be romantic, and here I have gathered together a number of starters, main courses and desserts which are bound to inspire your partner.

They utilize slightly more expensive ingredients than the recipes elsewhere in the book, and some of the techniques are more complicated, but none of them is too difficult or time-consuming. Most of the desserts can be prepared in advance, for instance, and there is no need to begin many of the main courses until you've finished your starter. This means both of you can sit down and eat in a relaxed fashion. It's up to you how much you want to impress your man or woman.

As this chapter is going down the sensual culinary route, a stuffed leg of turkey with roast potatoes, although great for Sunday lunch, doesn't really fit the bill. Instead, I've included a number of seafood dishes which are much lighter and healthier. Seafood is food for the brain, as well as the food of passion, so they say, and brain power and passion are both elements you might find you need during the course of your romantic evening.

There are also some chicken dishes. These are quite light as well, and the chicken with lobster, an idea culled from America, magnificently combines both fowl and seafood. I serve it with chips. You can never go wrong with chips!

To create good food, you need superb ingredients and flair. You must allow yourself time to prepare, and it's crucial that you buy the very best you can afford. As for the flair, I've tried to do all the hard work for you.

Don't forget about atmosphere: dim the lights, have plenty of candles lit on table and around the room, and put on the soft music of your choice. With that ambience, the food, and yourself, the evening should be a huge success.

Seared Scallop and Coriander Salad with a Lime and Red Pepper Dressing

10 large king scallops with corals, shelled

1 red pepper

Salt and freshly ground black pepper

Extra virgin olive oil

Juice and zest of 2 limes

2 x 15 g (½ oz) packets fresh coriander, half of it chopped

1 tablespoon red onion, chopped

250 g (9 oz) bag mixed salad leaves, pre-washed

Serves 2

Basically there are two types of scallop – queens and kings – and there is a great difference between them. King scallops are larger than queens and are diver caught. They provide a much more substantial piece of meat, but at a price. Steer clear of queens which are small, and after cooking end up looking like buttons. And never – repeat never – buy scallops that have been frozen: when defrosted and cooked they lose all their flavour, leaving a pan full of defrosted water to boot.

1 Pre-heat the oven to 200°C/400°F/gas mark 6. Cut the pepper in half, remove the seeds and stalk, and place in an ovenproof dish. Season with salt and pepper, drizzle with olive oil and place in the oven for 15 minutes until the skin has browned. Remove from the oven and while hot, place in a bowl, quickly cover with clingfilm and leave to go cold. When cold, remove and discard the skin.

2 For the dressing, cut the pepper flesh into small dice and place in a bowl with the lime juice and zest. Add 6 tablespoons of the olive oil with the chopped coriander and onion. Season and leave to one side.

3 Remove any black threads or sand from the scallops, but do not wash them. Heat a frying pan until very hot. Season the scallops with salt and pepper, place in the very hot pan and dry-fry on both sides for 30 seconds or until just cooked.

4 Combine half the dressing with the salad leaves and remaining coriander leaves, and place in two bowls. Divide the scallops between two plates. Finish the dish by drizzling the remaining dressing over the scallops, and serve with the salad.

James's tip

Any salad leaves would do, but the pre-washed bags are handy. The Continental selections normally contain a blend of frisée, radicchio and lollo rosso, while the Italian one adds rocket and herbs.

Pan-fried Mozzarella Wrapped in Bacon with Chutney and Sesame Seeds

1 x 150 g (5½ oz) ball buffalo Mozzarella cheese

4 slices speck bacon

4 tablespoons olive oil

Salt and freshly ground black pepper

100 g (3½ oz) mixed salad leaves

1 tablespoon balsamic vinegar

2 teaspoons sesame seeds, toasted

Plum chutney

8 plums, stoned and chopped

25 g (1 oz) butter

2 tablespoons caster sugar

3 tablespoons balsamic vinegar

Serves 2

This has always been very popular in my restaurants. My friends are keen on it too. One particular friend is always asking me to make it at his house, normally between three and four in the morning. As I'm never quite sober at that time, the fact that this recipe is easy is a point considerably in its favour.

Buy speck bacon, or Serrano ham instead, from delicatessens. Whichever you use, make sure it is cooked until crispy. And be sure to use buffalo Mozzarella, not one made from cow's milk, for maximum flavour.

1 Make the chutney in the morning. Melt the butter and sauté the plums for 2–3 minutes. Add the sugar and vinegar and simmer for 15–20 minutes until the plums are soft and the sauce is rich and sticky.

2 Open the packet of cheese, drain, and cut the cheese into four. Wrap each piece in a slice of speck, and secure with wooden cocktail sticks.

3 Heat half the olive oil in a non-stick pan until very hot. Season the wrapped Mozzarella, and fry for a few minutes on each side to brown and crisp the bacon.

4 Place the salad leaves in a bowl with the remaining olive oil, the vinegar and some seasoning, and mix. Divide between two plates in a high pile.

5 Remove the Mozzarella from the pan once the speck is nice and crisp, and place on top of the salad. Sprinkle with the toasted sesame seeds and pour over the juices remaining in the pan. Add the chutney to the side of each salad, and serve.

James's tip

To toast sesame seeds, put them in a dry pan with no oil and place on a moderate heat. Keep them moving in the pan to avoid burning. Toasting the seeds under a grill is not a good idea as they tend to burst open and go all over the place.

'A magical – and easy –
combination of soft
cheese, crisp bacon
and tart chutney…'

Thyme-steamed Mussels with Hot Sourdough Bread

900 g (2 lb) fresh mussels

25 g (1 oz) butter

½ red onion,
peeled and roughly chopped

3 garlic cloves,
peeled and roughly chopped

250 ml (9 fl oz) white wine

4 sprigs fresh thyme

250 ml (9 fl oz) double cream

Salt and freshly ground
black pepper

1 x 20 g (¾ oz) packet fresh
flat-leaf parsley, roughly
chopped

To serve

1 medium sourdough loaf

Butter

Serves 2

Here is a dish that is a bit like *moules marinières*, but with fresh thyme. Hot sourdough (or rye) bread is great to dunk in the juices afterwards

Mussels should be bought as fresh as possible. A mussel which is dead or even slightly bad can occasionally cause unpleasant side effects. Check them before cooking and discard any where the shells refuse to close when tapped briskly, as these are likely to be dead. Once they are cooked, throw away any that have not opened as they might also be bad. Also, avoid frozen mussels.

1 Wash the mussels in a colander to remove any dirt or grime. Pick through the mussels and remove the stringy bits from the edges; this is what the mussel uses to hold on to rocks or its mates before being taken from the sea. Discard any which do not close when tapped briskly.

2 Wrap the bread in foil (to prevent it from drying out) and place it in a low oven – about 150°C/300°F/gas mark 2 – to warm up slowly while you cook the mussels.

3 Place the butter in a large pan and sauté the onion and garlic for 1 minute before adding the wine. Bring to the boil and add the fresh thyme and mussels. Place the lid on the pan and cook for 3–4 minutes, until the mussels start to open.

4 Add the cream, salt, pepper and parsley, stirring the ingredients with a spoon. Heat through, making sure all the mussels are open (discard any that are not).

5 Divide the mussels between two bowls and pour the sauce left in the pan over them. Remove the bread from the oven and break into large chunks. I like to eat all the mussels first, and dunk the bread (with loads of butter on it) in at the end.

MAIN COURSES

Here we get a little more adventurous, and spend a little more money, but the recipes are still dominated by an intensity of flavour. The finished dishes look and taste great, but they're still not too difficult to achieve.

Baked Salmon and Dill Hash Brown with Pan-fried Tomatoes

1 shallot, peeled and chopped

1 garlic clove, peeled and chopped

Olive oil

1 large Estima baking potato

225 g (8 oz) salmon fillet (skin on but no bones)

1 egg, beaten

2 tablespoons fresh breadcrumbs

1 x 15 g (½ oz) packet fresh dill, chopped

Salt and freshly ground black pepper

3 plum tomatoes

Serves 2

To make it well, this dish needs lots of fresh dill and you must make sure you cook the potato through thoroughly before combining it with the salmon.

I've served the dish here with pan-fried tomatoes, but a Caesar Salad (see page 39) makes it a good complete summer dish. The egg is used to bind the mixture during cooking.

1 Pre-heat the oven to 200°C/400°F/gas mark 6. Place the shallot and garlic in a sauté pan with 4 tablespoons of oil and gently start to cook.

2 Peel the potato and cut it into 1 cm (½ in) dice, add to the pan and cook until the pieces are golden brown. Remove from the heat.

3 Cut the salmon into 1 cm (½ in) dice and place in a bowl with the egg, breadcrumbs and chopped dill, then pour on the potato, shallot and garlic. Mix well and season with plenty of salt and pepper.

4 Divide the mixture between two 7.5 cm (3 in) stainless-steel rings placed on an oven tray, pressing it in well. Place the tray into the oven and cook for 10 minutes.

5 Meanwhile cut each tomato into five slices and season with salt and pepper. Quickly seal in a hot pan with 1 tablespoon of olive oil to colour both sides. This should only take a minute or two.

6 Arrange the tomatoes on two plates, overlapping them into a circle pattern in the centre. Remove the salmon from the oven and place each ring in the middle of the tomatoes. Remove the metal rings. Drizzle with olive oil to finish the dish.

Red Mullet with Deep-fried Rocket and Toasted Sesame Seeds

2 x 175 g (6 oz) red mullet fillets (skin on but no bones)

Oil for deep-frying

115 g (4 oz) rocket leaves

Salt and freshly ground black pepper

2 tablespoons olive oil

25 g (1 oz) sesame seeds, toasted

Serves 2

Most fish, including red mullet, are available all year round, but the best season for this particular fish is from June or July to September. Avoid small fish which are fiddly to prepare and contain a lot of tiny bones. If you can't get larger fish, use salmon fillets instead as there really isn't much point in persevering with red mullet that are too tiny.

Serve the fish with plain boiled new potatoes. The simple flavours work together amazingly well. Alternatively, roast new potatoes in some garlic cloves, thyme, olive oil and rock salt for about 45 minutes on a high heat.

1 Place the red mullet fillets on a flat surface, skin side up, and with a sharp knife make about eight small slashes in the skin. Be careful not to cut through the whole width of the skin – leave about 5 mm (¼ in) on either side of the fillet.

2 Heat the oil in a deep pan or fryer to a high heat. Don't wash the rocket, but place it in the fryer in two batches: this is to prevent the fat from overflowing as, when you add the rocket, it will bubble up, so be careful. Keep your eye on the rocket and remove from the fryer once the leaves go translucent. Don't over-cook as the rocket will taste bitter; under-cooking will prevent the leaves crisping up. Once you have removed them from the fryer, place on some kitchen paper to drain, and season with a little salt.

3 Heat a non-stick pan to a high heat on the stove with the olive oil. Season the mullet fillets and place in the pan, skin side down, and cook for about 2 minutes, until the skin is nice and crispy. Then turn them over and cook for about 1 minute.

4 Divide the crisp rocket between two plates. Place the red mullet fillets, skin side up, in the middle of the rocket, sprinkle with some of the toasted sesame seeds. Serve.

Seared Tuna with Coriander Mash and Crispy Onions

2 x 140 g (5 oz) fresh
tuna steaks

Salt and freshly ground
black pepper

Olive oil

2 small white onions,
peeled and sliced into rings

Coriander mash

2 medium Estima potatoes

3 x 15 g (½ oz) packets
fresh coriander

1 garlic clove, peeled

Juice and zest of 2 limes

50 ml (2 fl oz) olive oil

75 ml (2½ fl oz) milk, hot

Serves 2

It was only when I went diving in the Maldives that I first experienced the taste of really fresh tuna. We barbecued it on the beach with fresh lime and coriander until it was still rare in the middle, and ate it off tin-lid plates sitting on the sand.

Tuna must be as fresh as possible, and cooked with the minimum of fuss to medium rare. Most supermarkets sell fresh tuna, but it is best to buy it cut to order from a fishmonger. It should be firm and a dark purple in colour.

1 Peel and quarter the potatoes and place them in a saucepan. Cover with water, add a good pinch of salt and bring to the boil. Cook until tender, then drain.

2 Place most of the coriander, the garlic and half the juice and zest of the limes in a blender. Blend with the olive oil to achieve a pesto-like purée. Season well.

3 Season the tuna steaks well and place on a hot griddle pan (see page 140) with a drizzle of olive oil. Cook for about 2 minutes on each side so that it is nice and pink.

4 While the fish is cooking mash the potato by hand with the milk. Mix in the coriander purée, and season.

5 In a hot pan, in about 4–6 tablespoons of olive oil, fry the onion rings until golden brown and crisp – a few minutes. Place on kitchen paper to drain.

6 To serve, arrange the mash in the centre of two plates, with the tuna on top. Cover with the crispy onions, and sprinkle over the remaining lime zest and juice, coriander leaves and a little pepper. Drizzle with olive oil and serve.

James's tips

When making mashed potatoes, always leave the drained potatoes to one side for a few minutes before mashing them. This allows the moisture to evaporate. If puréed too soon, the water still clinging to the potatoes will make the mash runny.

Use Estima potatoes, which are floury rather than waxy, making a very creamy purée. Using warm liquid helps to prevent lumps forming while puréeing the potatoes.

Parmesan Grilled Lobster with a Lime and Chilli Mayonnaise and Chips

1 x 675 g (1½ lb) cooked
lobster

Salt and freshly ground
black pepper

2 tablespoons mild
curry powder

1 x 15 g (½ oz) packet
fresh basil, chopped

8 tablespoons double cream

40 g (1½ oz) fresh
Parmesan, grated

2 large Estima potatoes,
peeled

Oil for deep-frying

Chilli mayonnaise

150 ml (5 fl oz) mayonnaise

Juice and zest of 1 lime

½ fresh large red chilli,
de-seeded and finely diced
(see page 137)

Serves 2

This dish, although impressive, is quick and easy. Basically it's just upmarket fish and chips – but on a lottery-winning scale. Although pre-cooked lobster is available, almost all year round, from many supermarkets, it tastes much better bought fresh and alive from a fishmonger.

1 Prepare the lobster by cutting it in half lengthways with a sharp knife. Take the legs off, and with a pair of nutcrackers or lobster crackers, open them up to remove the flesh. Place the flesh in a bowl. Remove the tail meat, slice and add to the claw meat. Remove the head meat and throw it away. Season the meat with salt, pepper and curry powder to taste, plus the chopped basil.

2 Place the meat back in the shells and pour the cream over. Top with the grated Parmesan, and leave to one side.

3 Mix the mayonnaise in a bowl with the lime juice, zest and diced chilli.

4 Heat the oil in a deep pan or fryer to a high heat. Cut the potatoes into large chips and cook for about 6–8 minutes until golden brown.

5 Meanwhile, place the lobsters under a pre-heated grill to colour the cheese.

6 Remove the lobsters from the grill and place on two plates. Serve the chips and the mayonnaise on the side.

Rockefeller Chicken with Lobster and Tomato Chips

2 chicken breasts
(free of bone, skin on)

1 x 450 g (1 lb) cooked lobster

Salt and freshly ground black pepper

Olive oil

1 x 190 g (6½ oz) jar pesto
(or home-made, see page 47)

1 x 200 g (7 oz) tin plum tomatoes

3 tablespoons chopped fresh parsley

2 tablespoons chopped celery

2 tablespoons chopped shallot

4 tablespoons chopped watercress

1 garlic clove,
peeled and chopped

3 tablespoons chopped fennel

3 tablespoons fresh white breadcrumbs

125 ml (4 fl oz) Pernod

2 tablespoons chopped fresh chives

2 tablespoons chopped fresh basil

2 tablespoons chopped fresh flat-leaf parsley

½ cucumber

Sprigs of fresh herbs

Tomato chips

225 g (8 oz) plum tomatoes

Serves 2

Here is the American idea of fish and meat together, taken further and combined with one of my favourite American sauces, Rockefeller. Usually served with oysters, its main flavours are Pernod, herbs and fennel.

The tomato chips have a strong intense flavour once the juices have been dried out.

1 The day before you want to serve the chicken make the tomato chips. Slice the tomatoes and arrange on grease-proof paper on a baking tray. Put into the oven at the very lowest heat possible (110°C/225°F/gas mark ¼, or less) and leave overnight or until the tomato slices are crisp. Cool and store in an airtight container.

2 Season the chicken breasts, then place in a frying pan with about 1 tablespoon of olive oil and cook.

3 Remove the shell from the lobster body and claws. Keep the lobster tail shell (cut in half lengthways) and the two antennae for garnish. Discard the remainder of the shell.

4 Purée the tinned tomatoes and place the pesto and the tomato purée into two small squeezy bottles.

5 Put the parsley, celery, shallot, watercress, garlic, fennel and half the breadcrumbs with another tablespoon of oil into a hot wok and cook for a second or two. Add 75 ml (2½ fl oz) of the Pernod and flame. Season quickly. Add the remaining breadcrumbs and the chopped herbs.

6 Cut the cucumber in half and remove the seeds. Slice lengthways on a mandoline to produce wide strips. Warm these through in one pan with a tablespoon of the Rockefeller sauce and a tablespoon of pesto, and warm the lobster flesh and tail shell pieces through in another pan with another tablespoon of oil. Pour the remaining Pernod over the lobster and flame.

7 Arrange the cucumber strips on the plates as a base. Cut the cooked chicken breasts into three slices each, and place on top, with the lobster flesh, and the lobster tail shell and antennae. Carefully squeeze the pesto and tomato purée on to the plates in a decorative pattern. Finish with a tablespoon of the Rockefeller sauce on the top. Garnish with tomato chips and sprigs of fresh herbs.

Crunchy Chilli Chicken
with Rocket Pesto

2 x 225 g (8 oz) chicken breasts

Salt and freshly ground black pepper

1 tablespoon olive oil

Topping

115 g (4 oz) instant *polenta*

2 plum tomatoes

¼ fresh red chilli, de-seeded (see page 137)

2 tinned anchovy fillets

¼ red pepper, de-seeded

¼ small red onion, peeled

½ garlic clove, peeled

2 tablespoons olive oil

Rocket pesto

115 g (4 oz) rocket leaves

½ garlic clove, peeled

1 tablespoon pine kernels, toasted

8 tablespoons olive oil

Serves 2

The 'crunch' here is created by the *polenta* topping on the chicken. The rocket pesto gives another kick to an already spicy dish, but it's great to really get the heart pumping.

I was nineteen when I first cooked for a girl, and this was the dish I made on our first date. It took me two hours to do the shopping; one and a half to do the cooking; I spent £50 on food, wine and flowers; and two hours and £200 on new clothes. All that hassle, and it turned out she was vegetarian. She ended up with meat-free pot noodles – and I ate it all.

1 To make the topping, place the tomatoes, chilli, anchovy, red pepper, onion and garlic into a blender and purée to a rough paste. Add the olive oil and season very well with salt and pepper. Combine this purée with all the instant *polenta* in a bowl.

2 Clean the blender and place all the pesto ingredients in it. Blend to a fine purée. Remove from the blender and leave to one side.

3 Pre-heat the oven to 200°C/400°F/gas mark 6. Season the chicken breasts with salt and pepper and seal in a hot pan with the olive oil for a few minutes on each side, to colour the flesh. Place the breasts on an oven tray and top each with a thick coating of the polenta mixture.

4 Bake in the oven for about 20 minutes, to cook the chicken through and allow the topping to go crunchy. If the chicken is cooked before the topping is crisp, remove from the oven and place under a pre-heated grill.

5 Place the breasts on plates, and serve with a dollop of the rocket pesto on the side.

Roast Marinated Duck Breast with a Chicory Tarte Tatin

2 x 200 g (7 oz) duck
breasts (with skin)

Salt and freshly ground
black pepper

Marinade
½ carrot,
scrubbed and grated

1 garlic clove,
peeled and chopped

½ red onion,
peeled and diced

55 g (2 oz) clear honey

50 ml (2 fl oz) white wine

3 tablespoons chopped fresh
coriander

2 tablespoons chopped fresh
mint

Juice and zest of 1 orange

4 tablespoons dark soy sauce

4 tablespoons sesame seeds

Chicory *tarte tatin*
4 heads chicory

250 ml (9 fl oz) orange juice

200 ml (7 fl oz) white wine

3 tablespoons chopped fresh
coriander

1 garlic clove,
peeled and finely chopped

55 g (2 oz) caster sugar

100 g (3½ oz) pre-rolled
puff pastry

Sauce
100 ml (3½ fl oz) white wine

115 g (4 oz) butter, softened

Serves 2

This is about as fussy as I get with food, but what a superb dish. The commonest breeds of duck are the Aylesbury and the Barbary; the Aylesbury has a lighter coloured flesh and is fattier. The French are now exporting duck breasts, and these are usually of good quality.

1 Put all the ingredients for the marinade in a china or earthenware bowl. Place the duck in it and leave for at least 2 hours – overnight is best.

2 Pre-heat the oven to 200°C/400°F/gas mark 6. Cut the chicory in half lengthways. Place in an ovenproof dish and pour on the orange juice and wine. Add the chopped coriander and garlic and season with salt and pepper, then cover with foil and place in the oven for about 20 minutes. Remove from the oven and take the chicory out of the juice, but keep the juice for later. Leave the oven on.

3 In a clean non-stick ovenproof pan, about 20 cm (8 in) in diameter, melt the sugar to a golden-brown caramel and place the drained chicory on top of this. Cut the pre-rolled puff pastry into a circle about 1 cm (½ in) bigger than the pan. Place the pastry on the top and tuck in the edges down the side of the pan to seal in the chicory. Place the pan in the oven and cook for 15 minutes, until the pastry is cooked.

4 Meanwhile, drain the duck, then place in a very hot dry pan. Seal on both sides, making sure the skin side is blackened slightly. Place the duck on an oven tray and roast in the oven for about 10 minutes, keeping it pink in the middle (about 12–13 minutes if you prefer it well done).

5 To make the sauce, put the juice from the chicory into a pan with the white wine and reduce until there's hardly any remaining. Turn the heat down and add the soft butter, bit by bit with a whisk, until you have a thickened sauce. Season and leave to one side.

6 Remove the duck and *tarte tatin* from the oven. Turn the *tarte* out while hot on to a large serving plate, inverting it so that the pastry is the base. Slice the duck thinly, place it on the *tarte*, spoon the sauce around and serve.

DESSERTS

Here are a few old and new favourites. Some have been subjected to the spun-sugar treatment, others to the introduction of new flavours which makes them fresher and more interesting. Most of them are for more than two servings, but left-overs are always tantalizing the next day.

Lemon, Pine Kernel and Brown Breadcrumb Cheesecake

2 egg yolks

4 tablespoons caster sugar

6 digestive biscuits

8 tablespoons brown breadcrumbs, freshly toasted

25 g (1 oz) butter, softened

1 tablespoon clear honey

Juice and zest of 2 lemons

1 tablespoon pine kernels, toasted

250 g (9 oz) mascarpone cheese

250 ml (9 fl oz) double cream, whipped to soft peaks

250g (9 oz) punnet fresh strawberries

Serves 4

The days of rock-hard cheesecakes topped with soggy tinned strawberries are dead and buried, I wish. This sort of thing is the new trend, an unusual combination of three diverse flavours.

I love this pudding – which I made up when appearing on *Ready Steady Cook* – as it's so simple and quick. The flavours of the pine kernels and lemon combine well with the cheese and breadcrumbs, but only use freshly toasted brown breadcrumbs.

1 Place the egg yolks and sugar into a bowl and whisk very well until light and thick (known as the light ribbon stage).

2 In another bowl, crush the biscuits finely. Add half the breadcrumbs, and combine with the softened butter and the honey. Place this mixture into four 7.5 cm (3 in) metal rings on a baking tray, or a 20 cm (8 in) springform tin, and press evenly over the base.

3 Add the lemon juice and zest, remaining breadcrumbs and the pine kernels to the egg mixture and mix together with a wooden spoon. Then fold in the cheese carefully followed by the whipped cream, being careful not to mix it too much as this will cause it to split and not set.

4 Spoon the mix into the tin(s) and, using a palette knife, press it down well to prevent air bubbles. Place in the fridge for about 1 hour to set.

5 Remove the flan(s) from the ring(s) or tin by wrapping around with a hot cloth to loosen the sides. Place the cheesecake(s) on a plate and decorate with the strawberries.

Lemon and Goat's Cheese Tart with Crème Fraîche

10 eggs

375 g (13 oz) caster sugar

500 ml (18 fl oz) double cream

Juice and zest of 5 lemons

10 g (¼ oz) (approx) butter, softened

225 g (8 oz) sweet pastry (bought will do)

55 g (2 oz) Gedi goat's cheese

Icing sugar

To serve

Crème fraîche

Serves 4

Lemon tart is highly regarded as a true chef's pudding, but it needs to be good: the pastry needs to be thin and the filling plentiful. My variation uses a very mild goat's cheese (see James's tip, page 44) which tends to balance some of the sharpness of the lemon juice.

1 To make the filling, crack the eggs into a bowl and whisk gently to break up the yolks. Add the sugar and continue to mix, then add the cream and the juice of the lemons – but not the zest. Pass the mixture through a sieve, then add the zest and leave to one side.

2 Pre-heat the oven to 200°C/400°F/gas mark 6. Grease a 20 cm (8 in) plain flan ring with the softened butter and place on a baking tray. Roll the pastry out until about 3 mm (⅛ in) thick. Carefully roll the pastry back on to the rolling pin, place over the ring, and unroll very loosely. (If you don't leave plenty of slack, the pastry will rip or shrink too much when cooking.) Carefully tuck the pastry down the sides of the ring, pressing into the bottom edge well, but be careful not to stretch or tear the pastry while doing so. Don't trim the pastry off, but line it with a circle of greaseproof paper that is bigger than the tart. Fill with either baking beans, rice or small wooden balls for baking blind.

3 Place in the oven and bake for about 10 minutes. Remove from the oven, remove the beans and paper, and place the pastry case back in the oven to colour the base. It should only take 3–4 minutes.

4 Turn the oven down to 140°C/275°F/gas mark 1. Pour the lemon mix into the pastry case, filling it to the top. Crumble the cheese over the tart, put back in the oven, and continue to cook for about 1–1½ hours until the filling is only just set.

5 Remove from the oven, trim off the edges of the pastry, and leave the tart to cool for about 2 hours.

6 Dust the tart with plenty of icing sugar and place under a hot grill to caramelize the top. Cut into wedges and serve with plenty of crème fraîche.

Cheat's Ten-minute Strawberry Gâteau

1 x 250 g (9 oz) sponge
flan case

600 ml (1 pint) double cream

25 g (1 oz) caster sugar

2 tablespoons (approx)
brandy

1½ x 250 g (9 oz) punnets
strawberries

55 g (2 oz) icing sugar

115 g (4 oz) mixed berries
(blackcurrants, blueberries,
redcurrants)

Few sprigs fresh mint

Spun-sugar topping

175 g (6 oz) caster sugar

Serves 4

This is one of my favourite desserts when cooking at home with only half an hour to spare. It looks as if you made it specially, but only minutes before you present it in all its glory it was a bought supermarket sponge flan.

1 Cut out the centre of the flan, using a 20–25 cm (8–10 in) stainless-steel ring (or the ring of a springform cake tin, without the base). With a sharp knife, carefully cut this sponge disc in half through the middle so you end up with two thin discs. Place the ring on a surface or tray, and put one of the discs inside it.

2 Whip the double cream with the sugar and brandy until thick. Keep in the fridge.

3 Hull the strawberries. Leave some whole for a garnish (about ten of the small ones), and cut the rest in half lengthways. Line the ring with the largest strawberry halves, cut side against the ring. You won't need all of them at this stage.

4 Spoon the chilled, whipped cream into the ring and gently press to the edges, keeping the strawberries in place against the sides. Arrange the rest of the halved strawberries over the top. Add the other sponge disc, and press it down. Dust generously with icing sugar. Lift the cake on to a plate. Remove the ring by carefully warming the edges with a hot cloth and lifting it straight off.

5 Place the sugar for the spun sugar into a very clean pan and heat. Once caramelized – golden brown and sizzling – remove from the heat to cool slightly.

6 While this is cooling, take a metal skewer and hold it in a gas flame until it is red hot. Use it to score the top of the gâteau in lines to create a diamond pattern. Decorate the top with the left-over strawberries and berries, and garnish with sprigs of fresh mint.

7 To finish, dip a small spoon into the caramelized sugar and twist it around a steel to create some sugar curls. Continue doing this until you have a candyfloss texture. Place this on top of the berries and serve.

White Chocolate, Whisky and Croissant Butter Pudding

500 ml (18 fl oz) milk

500 ml (18 fl oz) double cream

1 vanilla pod

3 whole eggs

5 egg yolks

200 g (7 oz) caster sugar

3 large croissants

25 g (1 oz) sultanas

25 g (1 oz) butter, melted

175 g (6 oz) good-quality white chocolate, grated

3 tablespoons whisky

55 g (2 oz) apricot jam, slightly melted

Icing sugar

Serves 4

My signature dish, I perfected this while working in London. It's ideal for using up slightly stale croissants or, better still, cheap ones from supermarkets near closing time. To be made well, it needs a good-quality white chocolate containing at least 40 per cent cocoa solids, good Scotch whisky and a combination of eggs and egg yolks (see James's tip).

1 Pre-heat the oven to 200°C/400°F/gas mark 6. Pour the milk and cream into a pan, add the vanilla pod, and gradually bring to the boil.

2 Place the eggs, egg yolks and sugar together in a bowl and mix well.

3 While the cream is heating, slice the croissants and place in an ovenproof dish, slightly overlapping the pieces. Sprinkle with sultanas and pour over the butter.

4 Once the cream has boiled, take it off the heat. Add the egg mixture and chocolate and stir well. Set on one side to allow the chocolate to melt, stirring occasionally.

5 Add the whisky to the cream mixture. Next, using a sieve, strain the cream over the croissants, cover with foil and bake in the oven for 15–20 minutes or until almost set.

6 Remove from the oven, coat the top with the jam, and dust with icing sugar. Caramelize the topping using a very hot grill or, if you have one, a blow torch (see page 140). This is best served at room temperature, with a spoonful of good ice-cream.

James's tip

The reason whole eggs are combined with egg yolks is that although the whites make the mixture tough, they're actually needed to make it set. The extra egg yolks makes the mixture more smooth and creamy. Please note that over-cooking the dish can make the custard curdle.

Sticky Toffee Pudding with Toffee Sauce

85 g (3 oz) butter, softened

25 g (1 oz) plain flour

175 g (6 oz) dark brown
demerara sugar

200 g (7 oz) pitted dried
dates

300 ml (10 fl oz) water

1 tablespoon golden syrup

2 tablespoons black treacle

2 eggs

½ teaspoon vanilla essence

200 g (7 oz) self-raising flour

1 tablespoon bicarbonate
of soda

Sauce

100 ml (3½ fl oz) double
cream

40 g (1½ oz) butter

40 g (1½ oz) dark brown
sugar

2 tablespoons black treacle

1 tablespoon golden syrup

To serve

Vanilla ice-cream

Serves 2–3

The king of all puddings, and my recipe is well over a hundred years old. It's not very slimming, mind you, but forget about diets and just enjoy yourself.

It can be made either in one 13 cm (5 in) pudding basin or, better still, two to three small 7.5 cm (3 in) metal pudding basins.

1 Preheat the oven to 200°C/400°F/gas mark 6. Take 25g (1oz) of the soft butter and butter the mould(s) very well. Scatter the plain flour over the buttered inside to coat it thoroughly. Discard any excess flour.

2 Using a food mixer with a bowl and a whisk attachment, blend the remaining butter and the demerara sugar.

3 While mixing, bring the dates and water to the boil in a small pan.

4 Add the golden syrup, treacle, eggs and vanilla essence to the butter mixture and carry on mixing. Then slowly add the flour on a slow setting. Once mixed together turn off the mixer.

5 Purée the water and date mixture in a blender, add the bicarbonate of soda, and quickly add this, while hot, to the egg and butter mix.

6 Once combined, pour into the mould(s) and bake in the oven for 20–25 minutes until the top of the pudding is just firm to the touch.

7 To make the sauce, place all the ingredients into a pan, bring to the boil, and it's ready.

8 Remove the pudding(s) from the mould(s) and place on a plate with lots of sauce on top. Ice-cream is a must when eating this dish, as crème fraîche isn't fat enough.

James's tip

The sponges and sauce can be made well in advance. In fact, the sponges can even be frozen. Both can be reheated in a microwave.

St-Emilion Chocolate and Macaroon Mousse

280 g (10 oz) good-quality plain chocolate, broken into pieces

85 g (3 oz) butter, melted

8 egg yolks

115 g (4 oz) caster sugar

4 egg whites

24 small macaroon biscuits

300 ml (10 fl oz) St-Emilion (or good Merlot)

Juice and zest of 1 orange

Serves 4

The famous wine town of St-Emilion has many good memories for me. My father often judges the wines of this area and he used to take me with him when visiting. I still go every September during the grape harvest.

St-Emilion is built on a hillside, and has the most beautiful town square with a church in the centre. Among the wine shops are *pâtisseries* selling the best macaroons I have ever tasted. The smell of cooking almonds drifts into my dad's house which overlooks the square. And if I'm honest, that's the real reason I go back – not for the wine.

This mousse is based on those macaroons and is seriously, seriously rich.

1 Place the chocolate in a bowl and melt either over a pan of hot water or, better still, in a microwave for 30 seconds. Stir in the melted butter.

2 In a blender, whisk the egg yolks and sugar together until light and thick (the ribbon stage), then pour into a large bowl.

3 Clean the blender bowl well and whisk up the egg whites stiffly. Leave to one side.

4 Take four large wine glasses and place three of the biscuits in the bottom of each. Pour half the wine into the bottoms of the glasses.

5 Stir the orange zest and juice into the sugar and egg mixture, and then quickly fold in the chocolate, then the egg white, very carefully.

6 Fill the glasses to halfway with this mousse mixture, and then top with the remaining biscuits. Pour the the rest of the wine over this and then fill the glasses up to the top with the rest of the mousse.

7 Place in the fridge for at least a few hours – preferably overnight.

dinners for two

breakfasts

The essence of good British food can be found in traditional British breakfasts, from Scotland's kippers and smoked haddock to Yorkshire black pudding, bacon and Cambridgeshire sausages.

Breakfast is known to be the most important meal of the day, but I also believe it can be the most tasty. One of my most vivid memories is of sitting around the kitchen table on a Sunday waiting for breakfast to be cooked by my mother and grandmother: the smell of bacon sizzling in the pan mingled with the aroma of beef already roasting in the Aga for lunch. Not a croissant in sight, but plenty of bread and dripping, sautéed kidneys or rabbit, black pudding doorsteps or faggots. New-laid eggs were fried in the fat left in the bacon pan, and came to the plate bright golden in the centre with the whites crisp and brown-frilled around the edges, like they should be.

I haven't let my nostalgia for Yorkshire mornings overwhelm me, though. You'll find a few old breakfast and brunch favourites here, but with a difference. I've transformed them all, to make classics with a twist: jugged kippers are served with a cider butter and spiked with lime; smoked haddock is poached with a hint of cinnamon; and scrambled eggs with green chilli will give you a real kick-start. The only dish that remains as tradition dictates is my all-time favourite, a bacon buttie, one of the best dishes ever. I've also included some fruity ideas for those who are not so keen on the Full Monty for breakfast, and given some unique and almost laughably easy recipes for fruit jams, as well as some drinks suitable for a late breakfast or brunch. However, many people like some carbohydrate in the morning, and there are plenty of suggestions from pancakes and waffles to chocolate *brioche* and an unusual chocolate cake. It's true that many of these are not entirely calorie-conscious, but who could resist chocolate cake with ice-cream on a relaxed Sunday (or any other) morning? I know I can't!

Poached Pears with Ice-cream and a Cinnamon and Goat's Milk Sauce

2 Comice pears

200 g (7 oz) caster sugar

1 vanilla pod

Juice and zest of 1 lemon

Sauce

600 ml (1 pint) goat's milk

200 g (7 oz) caster sugar

4 tablespoons golden syrup

1 cinnamon stick

1 teaspoon baking powder

To serve

200 g (7 oz) good vanilla ice-cream

Serves 2

There are no barriers in cooking food, so here I have abandoned tradition and the old-fashioned fruit salad, and gone for a seriously sweet and unhealthy pear dish with lots of ice-cream.

1 To make the sauce, place the milk, sugar and golden syrup in a heavy-based pan, and bring to the boil. Crumble the cinnamon stick into the milk and add the baking powder. Remove from the heat and stir well as the mix will rise very quickly. Continue to whisk the mixture until it stops rising, then place on the heat again and bring back to the boil, whisking all the time. Turn down the heat and simmer for about 45 minutes, stirring occasionally to prevent the mixture from burning.

2 Peel the pears, leaving the stalk on, and core them from the wide bottom. Place in a suitable pan with the sugar and vanilla and cover with hot water. Add the lemon juice and zest, and bring to the boil with the lid on. Turn down the heat and simmer for about 20–30 minutes until the pears are cooked, testing them with the point of a sharp knife to make sure they are soft.

3 When the sauce is ready, it should be a caramel colour (if it turns dark brown or black and burnt-looking, you weren't stirring enough).

4 Remove the pears from the pan and drain for a minute on some kitchen paper. Place the pears into a bowl, pour the hot sauce over the top and serve with the vanilla ice-cream on the side.

James's tip

When you add the baking powder to the hot milk and bring it back to the boil, you need to concentrate hard as it could burn very easily. Whisk continuously.

Banana and Allspice Tart with a Honey and Walnut Cream

1 x 350 g (12 oz) packet
frozen sweet pastry

3 bananas, peeled and diced

2 tablespoons ground
allspice

2 bananas, peeled and sliced

Icing sugar

100 ml (3½ fl oz) double
cream

50 ml (2 fl oz) clear honey

55 g (2 oz) shelled walnuts,
chopped

2 sprigs fresh mint

Serves 2

Bring this together at the very last moment, although the pastry circles could have been baked in advance (the day before, for instance). It'll take minutes only, while the tea or coffee is brewing, or your companion is squeezing some fresh orange juice.

Allspice is one of the great spices in cooking. It combines cinnamon, nutmeg and cloves and is often used in Caribbean food. It goes really well with bananas.

1 Pre-heat the oven to 180°C/350°F/gas mark 4. Roll out the pastry to 5 mm (¼ in) thickness, and cut into four 15 cm (6 in) circles. Bake in the oven for about 15 minutes, or until just brown on the edges only. Remove from the oven and allow to cool.

2 Mix the diced banana with the ground allspice and layer half of this mixture between two of the pastry circles. Make a second tart in the same way, using the other two circles of pastry.

3 Place the sliced banana on the top layers of pastry and dredge with icing sugar. Caramelize with a blow torch on the top (see page 142) or under a well pre-heated grill.

4 Whip the cream to soft peaks, then mix with the honey and nuts. Spoon on top of the caramelized pastry and banana, and garnish with fresh mint.

Char-grilled Peaches
with Amaretto and Basil

4 firm peaches

1 tablespoon olive oil

50 ml (2 fl oz) water

4 tablespoons caster sugar

1 vanilla pod, split in half

12 fresh basil leaves

50 ml (2 fl oz) Amaretto

2 tablespoons crème fraîche

Serves 2

Sexy or what! A combination of fruit and herbs sounds weird, but basil and Amaretto, an apricot and almond liqueur, go superbly with each other and with the slightly charred peaches to create an unusual alternative breakfast dish.

1 Heat up a griddle pan on a high heat (see page 142). Cut the peaches in half and remove the stones. Rub the oil over the cut sides of the flesh. Place the peaches, cut side down, on the griddle pan and cook for about 5–6 minutes without turning over.

2 Meanwhile, place the water, sugar and split vanilla pod in a pan and bring to the boil. Remove from the heat and allow the syrup to cool and thicken slightly.

3 Remove the peaches from the griddle and place on two plates, charred side up.

4 Rip the fresh basil leaves and add to the syrup, then pour over the peaches.

5 Heat the Amaretto, pour over the peaches and light with a match. When the flames have died down, spoon the crème fraîche into the middle of the peach halves.

118

'An Italian concept,
which makes for a
wickedly sexy breakfast'

Eggy Belffles™, Sautéed Tarragon Apples and Fromage Frais

2 Belffles™

200 ml (7 fl oz) milk

3 tablespoons caster sugar

2 eggs

2 Golden Delicious apples

2 sprigs fresh tarragon

40 g (1½ oz) butter

50 ml (2 fl oz) fromage frais

Serves 2

Belffle™ is a name for a type of Belgian waffle, which is available in some supermarkets. They are round in shape with a layer of caramel in the centre. They are a bit firmer in texture than ordinary waffles (which you can use instead, obviously), and hold together well in the egg mixture.

You could replace the fromage frais with soured cream or crème fraîche.

1 Put the milk, 1 tablespoon of the sugar and the eggs into a bowl. Using a whisk, mix the eggs in well, then leave to one side.

2 Cut the apples into four and remove the cores. Cut the remaining flesh into 1 cm (½ in) cubes. Chop the tarragon into fine pieces.

3 Put two frying pans on the stove and place half the butter in each. Add the apples and the remaining sugar to one, turn up the heat and leave to cook gently.

4 Meanwhile dip the Belffles™ well into the eggy mix and place in the other pan. Cook for about 2 minutes on each side until nice and brown.

5 Remove the Belffles™ from the pan and place on two plates with the sautéed apples piled up on top. Add 2 spoonfuls of the fromage frais, and serve hot with the creamy cheese just melting.

Hot Pancakes with Black Cherries, Berries and Vodka

Pancakes

115 g (4 oz) plain flour

1 egg

1 egg yolk

300 ml (10 fl oz) milk

2 tablespoons oil

Sauce

140 g (5 oz) black cherries

140 g (5 oz) blackberries
(or raspberries)

2 tablespoons caster sugar

Juice and zest of 1 orange

2 tablespoons cassis

4 tablespoons vodka

To serve

100 g (3½ oz) crème fraîche

Serves 2

To make pancakes, you need to use a heavy sauté pan, through which the heat will be conducted well. Fussy chefs say you should make the batter then rest it before cooking, but I think this rule only really applies to Yorkshire pudding batter. Here, as the mix doesn't need to rise, there's no point in resting it. Another tip is to make the pancakes with as little oil as possible.

1 To start the pancake mix, sieve the flour into a bowl and add the egg and egg yolk. Beat to mix before pouring the milk in slowly. This should prevent lumps forming.

2 Once the mix is smooth, heat a heavy sauté pan, crêpe pan or non-stick frying pan on the stove with a drip of oil in the bottom. Spoon either a small ladleful of the mix into the pan, or just enough to cover the base of the pan. As you put it in, lift the pan and move it in a circular fashion to ensure a thin layer of mix over the entire bottom. Return to the heat and colour on one side: about 2 minutes only. Turn or flip over and colour the other side, another couple of minutes. Remove the pancake from the pan and fold it in half and then in half again. Keep warm under foil on a large plate while you continue.

3 Make more pancakes in the same way until all the mix is gone. Keep them warm under the foil.

4 To make the sauce, put the cherries, blackberries, sugar, orange juice and zest into a pan. Place on a moderate heat and warm gently until the blackberries start to break up and so create a sauce in the bottom of the pan.

5 In the separate small pan quickly warm up the cassis and vodka, then flame them to remove the alcohol. As the flames die down, pour into the fruity sauce.

6 Uncover the pancakes, and pour the hot sauce over them. To finish, spoon the crème fraîche on top and allow it to melt slightly before you serve.

Hot Chocolate Brioche with Raspberry and Fig Jam

675 g (1½ lb) plain flour

1 scant teaspoon salt

75 g (2¾ oz) caster sugar

25 g (1 oz) fresh yeast

8 eggs, beaten

4 tablespoons cocoa powder

250 g (9 oz) butter, softened

50 g (2 oz) butter for greasing

1 egg yolk

To serve

Raspberry and Fig Jam
(see page 132)

Serves 6

The length of this recipe may be a little daunting, but good *brioche* is like good bread: it needs care, love and attention. The *brioche* is best made in a food mixer with a bowl, paddle and dough-hook attachment. And the jam needs to be made in advance.

Here, I have made a medium chocolate *brioche* by mixing a plain and a cocoa dough together, but if you are a chocoholic, you could use just a cocoa dough, doubling the amount of cocoa powder. Simply add the cocoa with the flour, then continue as in the recipe.

1 Sieve the flour, salt and sugar into the mixer bowl and crumble in the fresh yeast. Using the paddle or beater attachment, mix in the eggs slowly, bit by bit, until a dough is formed.

2 Mix the dough for a further 5 minutes, then take out of the bowl and divide into two. Put one half back into the machine and add the cocoa powder to it. Continue mixing the chocolate dough in the machine (with the dough hook now), and knead the other half by hand, for a further 2 minutes each. Place the doughs into two bowls, cover with two tea-towels, and place in a warm place for 20 minutes or until doubled in size.

3 Place the plain dough into the machine and on a low setting slowly add half the soft butter until it is all combined. Remove this buttery dough from the mixer, and do the same with the chocolate dough and the remaining soft butter.

4 Butter either an 18 cm (7 in) *brioche* mould or a 25 cm (10 in) loaf tin well and leave to one side. Turn both doughs out on to a cold board and knead together for 2–3 minutes to achieve a marbled effect. Place in the mould or tin, and return to a warm place to allow the mix to double again in size: about 20 minutes.

5 When risen, brush the dough with the egg yolk and cook in the oven pre-heated to 180°C/350°F/gas mark 4 for 45 minutes until golden brown but cooked in the middle. Cool, and serve sliced, fresh or toasted, spread with butter if you like and the cold jam.

Chocolate and Oil Cake with Hot Bananas and Lime Juice

Cake

20 g (¾ oz) butter

375 g (13 oz) plain flour

85 g (3 oz) cocoa powder

375 g (13 oz) caster sugar

2 tablespoons bicarbonate of soda

300 ml (10 fl oz) water

250 ml (9 fl oz) vegetable oil

25 ml (1 fl oz) white wine vinegar

Bananas

2 bananas

20 g (¾ oz) butter

Juice and zest of 1 lime

To serve

100 g (3½ oz) natural yoghurt

Serves 4 (and more)

This is a great recipe I learned from the famous Château Cheval Blanc in the hills of St-Emilion. It uses weird stuff such as vegetable oil, water and vinegar, and no eggs. It's the vinegar and soda that cause the cake to rise, but the grandmother of the house told me one golden rule: when the vinegar is added, the cake must be in the oven 30 seconds afterwards. Any longer than this and the mixture will fall when cooking, as it starts to rise even before it reaches the oven.

1 Butter a 20 cm (8 in) round cake tin and line it with buttered greaseproof paper. Pre-heat the oven to 180°C/350°F/gas mark 4.

2 Sieve the flour and cocoa powder into a bowl and add the caster sugar and bicarbonate of soda. Using a whisk, mix the water in slowly and then the oil. Once these are mixed in, add the vinegar quickly and pour the mixture into the cake tin. It looks rather like a soup – very runny – but don't worry about it.

3 Place immediately in the pre-heated oven for 30 minutes until cooked; it should still be a bit soggy in the middle. Remove from the oven and allow to cool.

4 Peel the bananas and place them on a small piece of foil. Add half the butter to each banana, and sprinkle the lime juice and zest over the top. Place under a pre-heated hot grill and cook for about 5 minutes until golden brown. Remove from the grill.

5 Arrange each banana on a plate with a chunk of the chocolate cake and a spoonful of yoghurt.

Hot Waffles with Sun-dried Tomatoes and Minted Cream

2 fresh waffles, about 35 g (1¼ oz) each

85 g (3 oz) crème fraîche

1 tablespoon chopped fresh mint

60 g (2¼ oz) butter, melted

6 sun-dried tomatoes in oil

Serves 2

Waffles should be bought fresh, not frozen, as the frozen ones tend to break and crumble when cooking, however carefully they've been thawed out. Good fresh ones are moist and require less butter, which makes them a little healthier.

This dish is very quick to make – about 10 minutes. It is also good as a quick lunch snack. But the waffles need to be served warm for the dish to work.

1 Place the waffles under a hot grill to colour both sides: a few minutes only.

2 Mix the crème fraîche and chopped mint together and leave to one side.

3 Remove the waffles from the grill, brush well with the melted butter and put on the plates. Spoon the minted crème fraîche on top, garnish with the sun-dried tomatoes and serve.

'I love to keep food simple, but I try to add to and create new and exciting flavours in individual dishes'

Scrambled Eggs with Green Chilli and Crispy Serrano Ham

6 medium eggs

Salt and freshly ground black pepper

½ fresh green chilli

6 slices Serrano ham

25 g (1 oz) butter

100 ml (3½ fl oz) double cream

Serves 2

A good scrambled egg should be both creamy and light, not the standard school-dinner style of *blancmange* pellets floating in water. To make them well you need to be at the stove all the time, not wandering off elsewhere. The secret is to add the cream halfway through cooking the eggs as this will prevent them from over-cooking.

I have used chilli here for an added kick to the flavour, but you can leave it out if you wish.

1 Place a sauté pan on the stove and heat it up on a medium heat. Pre-heat the grill as well.

2 Break the eggs into a bowl and season well with salt and pepper. Remove and discard the seeds from the chilli, and dice the flesh up very finely. Place the ham on a grill tray and put under the pre-heated hot grill to crisp up; it will only take a few minutes.

3 Add the butter to the sauté pan, heat slightly, then pour in the eggs. Quickly mix the eggs with a whisk and, when half cooked, add the cream, whisking all the time.

4 Just as the eggs are beginning to set, remove from the heat, correct the seasoning and quickly place on to warm plates. Serve with the hot crisp ham and sprinkle with the chopped green chilli.

Black Pudding with Caramelized Apple and Cider

175 g (6 oz) black pudding,
cut into 1 cm (½ in) slices

1 Golden Delicious apple

55 g (2 oz) butter

1 tablespoon caster sugar

50 ml (2 fl oz) cider

Salt and freshly ground
black pepper

Serves 2

The fact that black pudding is made from pig's blood mixed with oatmeal, suet and onion may not appeal to you, but I consider it one of the true essentials in breakfast cooking. The best come from good butchers' shops, as they are usually made fresh on the premises. These have much more flavour and taste than the commercial, branded black puddings.

I believe black puddings should be sliced and pan-fried. The cooking time is important as well as the heat of the pan, and you don't need much fat. A cooked slice of black pudding should be slightly crisp on the edges but moist in the centre.

1 Place two frying pans on the stove and heat up to a high heat while you prepare the apple. Core the apple whole, then cut it in half and slice each half into five slices.

2 Divide the butter between the two pans, and put the sugar in one of them. Place the black pudding into the non-sugared pan, reduce the heat and cook for 2–3 minutes, turning occasionally.

3 When the sugar and butter in the other pan have started to turn golden brown, add the apple slices. Turn up the heat and quickly caramelize the apple: about 3 minutes. Pour in the cider to deglaze the pan, stirring well, and season quickly with salt and pepper.

4 To serve, either put the apple mixture and the black pudding into separate bowls or plates for the two of you to help yourselves from, or arrange the black pudding on the two plates with the apple on top.

Jugged Fresh Kippers with Cider Butter and Lime

2 fresh kippers

100 g (3½ oz) butter, softened

3 tablespoons fresh parsley, chopped

¼ apple, grated

50 ml (2 fl oz) cider

Juice and zest of 1 lime

Serves 2

When I was about eight years old, my family had a holiday house in a small and beautiful village called Robin Hood's Bay near Whitby in North Yorkshire. Whenever we visited Whitby, all the other kids would either climb the 150 steps to the castle to see the Tomb of Count Dracula, or spend their pocket money at the amusements on the pier.

I would spend the entire day watching the fishing boats go in and out of the harbour, and would invariably park myself next to the open window of a fish smokery. My mum would object vociferously as we travelled back in the car: I smelt like an old kipper.

This is a very quick and simple dish that should take only a few minutes.

1 Place the kippers in a tall jug with the tails sticking out of the top, and carefully pour boiling water into the jug, up to the top.

2 Place the softened butter in a bowl and mix first with the chopped parsley, then more slowly with the grated apple and cider. Leave to one side.

3 After the kippers have been in the water for about 2–3 minutes, pour off the water and place the kippers, first on kitchen paper to dry, and then on plates.

4 Put half the butter on to each kipper along with the juice and zest of the lime. Eat as is, or with some sliced bread.

Cinnamon Poached Smoked Haddock with Fried Green Tomatoes

**4 green tomatoes
(or unripe, firm tomatoes)**

300 ml (10 fl oz) milk

¼ cinnamon stick

1 bay leaf

**2 x 140 g (5 oz) pieces
smoked haddock**

100 g (3½ oz) butter

**Salt and freshly ground
black pepper**

**1 tablespoon chopped fresh
parsley**

Juice of ½ lemon

Serves 2

Smoked haddock is a traditional food, but has been subjected to a few small changes over the years. One of these was the introduction of bright yellow, dyed, smoked haddock. If you can find it, the real smoked haddock is far superior. It is slightly more expensive, is a creamy colour, not yellow, and will have a deeper, smokier smell. It's normally sold as 'naturally smoked haddock'. Use it fresh (don't freeze it), but it will be fine in the fridge for a few days.

Most people don't associate fish with spices, but fresh cinnamon and naturally smoked haddock go really well together. Try it and see.

1 Cut the tomatoes into thickish slices: roughly about 4 slices per tomato.

2 Place the milk, cinnamon and bay leaf into a pan with the fish and cover with a lid. Bring to the boil and simmer slowly for about 2–3 minutes, depending on the thickness of the fish. Turn the heat off, remove the lid and leave to stand while you cook the tomatoes.

3 Melt half the butter in a sauté pan, add the tomatoes and season with salt and pepper. Sauté quickly until golden brown, then remove the slices from the pan and divide between two plates.

4 Return the pan to the heat and add the remaining butter, the chopped parsley, lemon juice and seasoning.

5 Remove the fish carefully from the milk in the pan, using a slotted fish slice. (Discard the milk.) Place the fish on top of the tomatoes, pour over the remaining juices from the sauté pan, and serve.

Bacon Buttie

8 rashers streaky
smoked bacon

4 slices bloomer bread
or *pain de campagne*

30 g (1¼ oz) dripping

40 g (1½ oz) butter

2 fresh tomatoes, sliced

Freshly ground black pepper

Serves 2

There is nothing better, in my opinion, than the smell of bacon cooking. But a real bacon buttie must be made with the best, smoked streaky bacon money can buy, and lots of butter.

Nigel Slater, one of the true greats when it comes to simplifying dishes, discusses his approach to the bacon sandwich in one of his books, and his ideas are along much the same lines as mine: the bacon should be crisped in a pan with butter, and not grilled; the bread should be briefly fried in the bacon fat with a bit more butter; the buttie is then built up with some grilled tomatoes, the fried bread and some freshly ground black pepper.

You could also use mustard or tinned tomatoes, but it must always be really good-quality bacon. However it even tastes great with standard, white, sliced supermarket bread!

1   Heat a large frying pan: melt and heat the dripping.
2   Add the bacon, watching out for fat spitting out at you. Fry until nice and crisp then remove from the pan. Add the butter to the pan.
3   Fry the slices of bread on one side in the fat and butter for a minute or two only, just so that they soak up the juices.
4   Place two pieces of bread, fried side up, on the plates. Build up the buttie with the bacon and sliced fresh tomatoes. Season with pepper. Pour over any other juices from the pan, top with the other slice of bread, fried side down, and serve.

JAMS

Jam-making is a long-established British tradition with many secret recipes and methods handed down from generation to generation. Here are a few alternatives – I don't think too many grannies would have thought of them!

I've given the basic method in the first jam. Do the same with all the others. They're very easy, although a jam thermometer will help.

Raspberry and Fig Jam

600 g (1 lb 5 oz) granulated sugar

6 fresh ripe figs, chopped

450 g (1 lb) raspberries

300 ml (10 fl oz) water

This is good served with the Hot Chocolate Brioche on page 122.

1 Place the sugar on an oven tray and warm it in a cool oven, at 140°C/275°F/gas mark 1.
2 Put the figs, skin and all, in a pan with the raspberries and water. Simmer over a low heat until the fruit starts to break up and becomes like a purée.
3 Add the sugar and a sugar thermometer. Bring to the boil and boil quickly until the temperature reads 104°C/220°F. Alternatively, see James's tips.
4 Remove from the heat and cool for about 20 minutes before pouring into clean jam jars. Put the lids on and store in a cool place.

James's tips

Heating up the sugar speeds up the cooking process, as warm sugar dissolves more easily.

If you haven't a sugar thermometer, put four small saucers in the freezer compartment of your fridge before you start. When you have boiled the jam for the required time – about 15–20 minutes – pour a teaspoonful on to one of the cold saucers, and leave for a second or two. If a crinkly skin has formed when you push it with your finger, the jam has reached setting point. If not, boil for another 5 minutes and test again.

Plum and Sage Jam

675 g (1½ lb) caster sugar

900 g (2 lb) fresh plums,
stoned and roughly chopped

200 ml (7 fl oz) water

10 fresh sage leaves,
ripped up

2 pinches powdered cinnamon

Add the sage and cinnamon when the jam has cooled, stirring them in well.

Peach and Saffron Jam

800 g (1¾ lb) caster sugar

900 g (2 lb) peaches,
stoned and roughly chopped

1 tablespoon powdered
pectin

250 ml (9 fl oz) water

Pinch of saffron strands

Add the saffron as the jam is cooling. Some fruit lacks the natural pectin that helps jam to set, so powdered has to be added with the sugar. (You'll find it in health-food stores and good supermarkets.) Pectin-rich fruits include apples, berries, pears and lemons.

Saffron has a unique flavour and a rich yellow colour. Just a pinch is enough because of its strength. Saffron strands are better than the powdered version and give a much richer colour.

Vodka, Basil and Lemon Jam

900 g (2 lb) caster sugar

Juice of 10 lemons

Zest and flesh of 7 lemons
(no pith), chopped

75 ml (2½ fl oz) vodka

200 ml (7 fl oz) water

55 g (2 oz) fresh basil leaves,
ripped

Add the basil leaves when the jam has cooled.

Strawberry and Black Pepper Jam

800 g (1¾ lb) caster sugar

900 g (2 lb) fresh strawberries

Juice and zest of 2 lemons

200 ml (7 fl oz) water

2 tablespoons cracked black
peppercorns

Add the black peppercorns while the jam is cooling.

DRINKS

Here's a selection of drinks that you might enjoy having with a special brunch as well as, or instead of tea or coffee.

Spiced Bloody Mary

4 tablespoons vodka

1 x 200 g (7 oz) tin plum tomatoes

3 dashes Worcestershire sauce

½ teaspoon horseradish sauce

3 dashes Tabasco sauce

Pinch each of salt, caster sugar and black pepper

8 ice cubes

Serves 2

Not really to be drunk before 11am, but good to spice you up and set you on the way for the day ahead. Brilliant for hangover mornings!

1 Simply put all the ingredients, apart from the ice, into a blender. Blend until all the ingredients are well mixed.
2 Divide the ice between two tall glasses, pour the mix over the top, and serve.

Black Velvet

A mixture of equal parts of champagne and Guinness: say, 250 ml (9 fl oz) of each.

Cranberry Juice with Champagne

A slightly more refined and fruitier mix than the one above, but made in just the same way, with equal amounts of champagne and fresh cranberry juice.

Rum and Hot Chocolate

This is a brilliant winter warmer, but it must be made with a good-quality French variety of drinking chocolate, usually available in the special selection aisles of supermarkets. Such varieties are slightly more expensive because they use a higher percentage of cocoa mass.

Make it up with hot milk as described on the packet, then pop in some dark rum to taste. You could add some cocoa powder and sugar for a richer drink. And, to make it even more special, leave the chocolate to cool a little and lightly whip up some double cream. Spoon on to the top of each cup to resemble a cappuccino.

ingredients & equipment

Good ingredients and equipment lie at the heart of good cooking and good eating. In this chapter, I give you a brief run-down on my approach to buying a selection of fresh and store-cupboard products, and a hint or two about equipment.

INGREDIENTS

Meat

The way we shop today has had a drastic effect on the production of meat. Sadly, there is a demand for minimum fat, maximum meat and quick growth. This applies to lamb, pork, beef and poultry. Because of bulk ordering and buying, small butchers are dying out, and it was really only in their shops that meat was hung properly. Consumer sources other than butchers require too fast a turnover for this to be such a priority.

In my opinion, there should be a butcher's shop on every corner as there was twenty years ago. A good local butcher can come to know your tastes, order things specially, and will be happy to turn a best end of lamb into a crown roast free of charge. It's good, though, that some supermarkets are introducing fresh meat counters, where the cuts are not bright red and sweatily encased in clingfilm. If you can find a good butcher, you will be assured of good meat.

Seafood

Fish is one of the best foods in the world: quick and simple to cook, with flavours more variable than fruit. But buying good fish can be a bit hit and miss, as good-quality fishmongers are disappearing as fast as butchers. Whether buying from a shop, or a supermarket fish counter, look for bright colours, bright not sunken eyes, a slimy skin, not dry or damp. A fresh fish should smell of sea, air and water – not fishy. Ask the fishmonger to scale, gut and fillet your fish – it's his job, after all.

Size is important: a small red mullet is all bones, and a thin cod fillet will break up in cooking. Bigger is better. And the same applies to shellfish: you may think you're saving money buying small lobsters or scallops, but after cooking you'll be left with virtually nothing to eat. (On average, there is some 60 per cent wastage when cooking a lobster.)

If possible, buy shellfish live: the shells of live oysters, mussels and scallops should be closed. Live lobsters and crabs should be moving quickly, not sluggishly.

Vegetables

As standards in supermarkets improve, their vegetables are as good as those at market stalls and in greengrocers. Large supermarket chains now have the ability to buy their produce throughout the world, and can have a green bean that was grown in Kenya delivered to the UK within twenty-four hours. There are some superb individual shops and market traders, however, many of which have been around for generations.

There are no general golden rules about buying vegetables: just your instinct, and touch, feel and colour, all of which can indicate freshness.

For health, most vegetables are best eaten raw, or cooked as minimally as possible. Wash well, prepare and cook quickly, as nutrients deteriorate rapidly. Cook in very little water, as most of the nutrients, particularly those in green vegetables, are water soluble. This will retain maximum flavour as well.

Fruit

Gone are the days when there were just oranges and a couple of apple varieties on greeengrocers' shelves in winter. Now we have fresh lychees, mangos and pawpaws, brought here from all ends of the earth. Although I am not a lover of many of these, as their flavour and value for money can be questioned, I think exotics should be bought from supermarkets. Indigenous fruit, such as berries, should only be bought in season direct from the grower or from a reliable local greengrocer.

Fruit should be eaten raw on the whole, although some gain interesting flavours and textures when cooked. Wash and dry them first. If they need to be prepared, cut and eat quickly as colour and nutrients might be lost.

Spices, Salt and Pepper

Spices are normally bought in two basic forms, fresh whole or ground. I prefer to use fresh whole, as once a spice is ground its essential oils, and therefore its flavour, dissipate very quickly. However, some spices cannot successfully be ground at home: mace and cinnamon, for instance. Ginger is available as a fresh root, and this must be peeled and grated or chopped very finely, and used with caution because of its strength.

Salt and pepper are the most essential flavour enhancers in cooking. I use rock salt (literally from rock, from ancient dried-out saline lakes), and sea salt (collected from salt pans, where seawater has evaporated). I like to use the crystalline forms of both loose in the kitchen, and grind them from a grinder at the table. The pepper I use is black, whole peppercorns, freshly ground from a mill; not powder, as this has a poor taste and is nothing like real ground black pepper.

It is important to bear in mind the difference between various types of red chilli. Generally speaking, the larger a fresh (or dried) chilli is, the milder its flavour tends to be. To de-seed, carefully slit open along the length, and then scrape out seeds and pith. Chop flesh as specified in the recipe. Always remember to make sure you wash your hands very thoroughly after handling chillies.

Pasta

The Italians' true passion, followed by cars and fashion. Many households there make their pasta fresh, but quite a number of restaurants use dried. Choose good-quality dried egg pasta, which comes in many shapes and sizes. As a good-quality dried pasta is better than a poor- or medium-quality fresh one, I prefer plain pasta flavoured with a sauce, not the ravioli-style or coloured pastas available in many shops.

To cook, follow the instructions given on the packet.

Rice

For risotto, you must use an Italian rice such as *arborio*, *carnaroli* or *vialone*, as these types take up the most amount of liquid. They need to be stirred so that the grains do not stick together.

Basmati and Thai fragrant are the best long-grain rice varieties, and obviously the first choice for any type of Indian or oriental dish.

When cooking rice, always follow the instructions on the packet.

Oils

Oils are the chef's best tool; they're his or her cooking medium and they often add considerable flavour.

Vegetable oils, such as sunflower, soya or corn, should be used for deep-frying and shallow-frying, or in dishes where little or no oil flavour is required (they are virtually flavourless).

Olive oils vary in intensity of flavour, colour and expense. The first and second pressings of olives yield extra virgin and virgin olive oils, which are so wonderful that you must use them only for dressings and for drizzling over a dish. The third pressing gives olive oil which is still of good quality, but can be used as a general-purpose cooking medium as well as in dressings to which a lot of other flavours have been added.

Nut and seed oils, such as walnut, hazelnut and sesame, are classed as aromatic oils by chefs because their flavours are so strong. Although they are quite expensive, use them for dressings and for drizzling over a dish as a final touch. These oils go rancid very quickly, so are best stored in the fridge.

The very special properties of truffle oil are mentioned on page 38.

Vinegars

Vinegars, like oils, vary in strength, flavour and price, from twenty-year-old balsamic to pickling vinegar. It is vital to use each one in its appropriate form of cooking.

Vinegar is the result of the souring of an alcohol, whether red or white wine, sherry, beer or cider (and rice wine in Asia). Wine vinegars can be used in both dressings and in cooking. They should be cooked out – reduced to an essence – not added at the last minute. Balsamic vinegar has a flavour smoother and deeper than other vinegars, as it is fermented slowly in wooden barrels, from grape juice rather than alcohol, sometimes over many years. Good balsamic vineger should be at least three years old.

I love to use it in both cooking and dressings, and as a last-minute addition to something such as a beef stew, it is a great flavour enhancer.

Convenience or ready-prepared foods

I'm not talking here of ready-prepared dishes or meals, although the quality of these has risen sharply since some chefs have left restaurant kitchens to work for food manufacturers.

I'm talking about foodstuffs that are packeted, jarred, tinned or frozen, things that many chefs and cooks would avoid, but which can, if chosen and used judiciously, be very useful and tasty. The fact that they also save time is central to my culinary philosophy.

One of the best ready-made products for home cooks is the fresh stock now sold in supermarkets. This saves hours of simmering and reducing. Another item which should be a constant in the store cupboard is plum tomatoes in tins. Often these are better than the real thing in terms of flavour and colour. Tinned pulses, such as chickpeas and lentils, are also excellent and convenient, as are tinned salmon, tuna and anchovies.

I use a number of foods in jars, and pepperonella (see page 35) is a favourite. Olives, sun-dried tomatoes in oil and certain pestos are good too. Be careful with a pesto: choose those which are greenest in colour, as these use the leaf only, rather than the whole plant.

Other handy foods are frozen pastry, such as filo and puff pastry, broad beans and peas. The latter two are often just as good, if not better, than fresh. From experience, I know that large frozen food companies can strip a field of peas, bag and freeze them within about two hours. Your local greengrocer couldn't guarantee that sort of freshness. (But, that said, there's nothing quite like raw peas eaten straight from the pod.)

EQUIPMENT

You don't need much equipment in the home kitchen, but what you do have must be of good professional quality.

Pans

If you cook a lot, black cast-iron pans are best as they are robust and distribute heat well. They may not look wonderful, but they will do their job and last well. Choose pans with metal handles that can go from hob to oven. If in doubt, buy one pan and try it out, rather than buying a whole set at once. Expensive pans aren't necessarily the best. Griddle pans are very useful for charring meat and fish. But when buying one, do be careful. The best are square, with straight griddle marks, and the ridges or grooves should be quite deep. The whole idea of griddling is to have the meat or fish sitting above the fat.

Knives

Knives are essential in the kitchen, and I've had mine for twenty years. (I was given them when I was very young!) The best have moulded plastic handles (wood tends to split after a while). I prefer a high-quality German- or Swiss-made knife, but knives are usually bought according to personal preference as no set is the same.

To sharpen them, use a diamond steel; mine doubles up as a tool for spun sugar.

Blenders and mixers

I'm a fan of the small electric hand blender, which is great for soups and sauces. Electrical mini choppers are good for purées and pastes such as pesto. The only recommendation I can give about larger machines such as blenders, mixers or processors is that they should be made from metal, as they will last longer.

I've mentioned blow torches a few times in dessert recipes. You won't find these in kitchen shops; buy them in your local hardware shop. If you don't trust yourself with one – they are quite dangerous – simply put the dessert under a hot grill to achieve the same effect.

Chopping boards

These are vital. In an ideal world, we'd all chop on wood, but with health risks in mind, there are now some very good plastic boards available. They also come in a range of colours, so that it's easy to set them aside for different uses and different ingredients.

Small utensils

Other small pieces I use a lot are a speed potato and vegetable peeler (just the job for shaving Parmesan as well), and a mandoline for thin slices. Mandolines must be made from metal, not wood or plastic, as these tend to bend while they are being used and can cause a nasty cut.

INDEX

AUTHOR ACKNOWLEDGEMENTS

In particular I would like to thank Margaret Little and Mitchell Beazley for giving me the chance to write my first book and Susan Fleming, for all her work making sense of my recipes and for coping with my dreadful spelling. I would also like to thank Fiona Knowles, Jeremy Hopley, Catherine Rowlands and Wei Tang for making the food look ace and making me look respectable at that time in the morning; and Claire Bressano for her help in testing and eating my recipes.

Thanks also to Mary Ramsay, Fern Britton and the team on *Ready Steady Cook*; to Trish Cannain at Action time for spotting me in the first place.

Thank you to all those who have given me a job, to Pierre Chevillard at Chewton Glen and Phillip Howard at The Square; to Robin and Gerard at the Hotel du Vin for giving me the chance to be head chef, making me work my backside off and letting my ideas run free.

Finally thanks to my ex-girlfriends for dumping me and letting me get on with cooking. Cheers and special thanks to Alex, the best mate anyone could have, and to Liz Mariner.